Uniform Commercial Code—
Article 9

Uniform Commercial Code— Article 9

Problems and Materials on Secured Transactions

Robert J. D'Agostino
PROFESSOR OF LAW
ATLANTA'S JOHN MARSHALL LAW SCHOOL

with
Matthew C. Dials

CAROLINA ACADEMIC PRESS
Durham, North Carolina

Library of Congress Cataloging-in-Publication Data

D'Agostino, Robert J.
  Uniform commercial code, Article 9 : problems and materials on secured
transactions / Robert J. D'Agostino.
      p. cm.
  Includes bibliographical references and index.
  ISBN 978-1-61163-362-7 (alk. paper)
  1. Security (Law)--United states. 2. Uniform commercial code. Secured
transactions. I. Title.

  KF1050.D34 2012
  346.73'0666--dc23   2012036491

CAROLINA ACADEMIC PRESS
700 Kent Street
Durham, North Carolina 27701
Telephone (919) 489-7486
Fax (919) 493-5668
www.cap-press.com

Printed in the United States of America

Contents

Table of Cases

Preface

Robert D'Agostino is a Professor of Law at Atlanta's John Marshall Law School located in Atlanta, Georgia. During his tenure at John Marshall, he served as Dean from 1996 to 2000. Professor D'Agostino practiced bankruptcy and commercial law between careers in academia. Prior to joining John Marshall in 1995 and after practicing law for some 15 years, Professor D'Agostino was a tenured professor at what is now Widener Law School in Delaware. In 1981 through 1982, he took a leave of absence from Widener to serve as a presidential appointee to the U.S. Department of Justice under President Ronald Reagan, where he served as an Assistant Deputy Attorney General for Civil Rights. He earned a B.A. and M.A. from Columbia University before working his way through Emory Law School where he earned a J.D. while teaching high school science followed by employment as a social worker. His publications deal with topics related to bankruptcy, civil rights, and constitutional law. An avid bicyclist, "Dag" is also a political activist.

Acknowledgments

Assisted by Matthew C. Dials, Atlanta's John Marshall Law School Class of 2012.

Further assistance was provided by Latrice E. Thomas, Atlanta's John Marshall Law School Class of 2013.

Prof. D'Agostino extends a special thank you to Michael Lynch, Director of the Law Library and Professor of Law at Atlanta's John Marshall Law School for proof reading and suggesting changes to the manuscript.

Note

These materials are based on the current version of Article 2 and the 2001 version of Article 9. Appendix B contains a Summary Collateral Index. Insofar as Georgia has adopted non-uniform amendments to Article 9, selected sections are included as Appendices C and D.

Unless Otherwise Stated, all references are to code sections contained within the Uniform Commercial Code, copyrighted by the American Law Institute and the National Conference of Commissioners on Uniform State Laws.

Uniform Commercial Code— Article 9

Chapter One

Basic Concepts

A. Introduction

1. The Importance of Secured Transactions

Unlike a sale, a secured transaction usually involves three actors—the Debtor, the Secured Creditor, and the Finance Company. Of course, if a Secured Creditor sells on credit, a Finance Company is not involved, at least not initially.

As you study Article 9 be particularly aware of the definitions of *security interest, lien, obligor, debtor, creditor*, and the processes giving rise to *attachment, perfection*, and *priority* of security interests. Those processes and the rights of competing creditors may be affected by whether the transaction involves a merchant, a consumer, or a non-merchant businessman and whether the buyer of a good is a buyer-in-the-ordinary course (BIOC).[1]

Note that much of the litigation involving the effectiveness and priority of security interests arises in the context of bankruptcy. A person, defined in § 1-201(30) to include an individual or an organization, filing for bankruptcy is generally insolvent under one of the three tests for insolvency which include the failure to pay debts in the ordinary course of business, cannot pay debts when they become due and insolvent within the meaning of the federal bankruptcy law. *See*, § 1-201(23) and Comment 23 to that section. These tests are often summarized as the balance sheet test (liabilities exceed assets) or the equity insolvency test (cash flow inadequate to meet obligations as they become due).

A creditor with a priority security interest will get repaid or realize on the security interest before a creditor with a lower priority security interest. The

---

1. Note that the term "buyer-in-the-ordinary course" is abbreviated to BIOC in practice and within the textbook.

trustee in bankruptcy, whose existence is presumed upon the filing of a bank-ruptcy petition, is often referred to as the "enemy of the secured creditor," be-cause the trustee's duty is to maximize the debtor's bankruptcy estate available for distribution. The trustee may seek to increase the estate available to the unsecured creditors by avoiding security interests.

Most students are familiar with the concept of granting a creditor an inter-est in property. Although Article 9 does not apply to real estate, the concept of a lending institution granting a mortgage[2] subject to foreclosure upon default is analogous to a creditor's right of repossession of collateral under Article 9. Like a mortgage, a security interest is an interest in property. *See,* § 1-201(37).[3]

Generally, the creation of a security interest in favor of a lender generally in-volves three documents, which include the following:

    a. **Monetary obligation:** A debtor's obligation to make periodic pay-ments, usually a possessory note.

    b. **Security Agreement:** An agreement in which a debtor grants a credi-tor an interest in a debtor's personal property.

    c. **Financing Statement (UCC # 1):** A financing statement is filed to give notice to third parties, that is, parties not involved in the transaction that there is a party that may have an interest in personal property of the debtor.

What constitutes a security agreement and what notice may substitute for a fi-nancing statement shall be covered in the following material.

*Study Tip: As you progress through this book, it will be beneficial for you to fol-low and apply the steps found in **Approaching Article 9 Analytically,** Appendix A.*

Questions

Problem 1.1

➢ Explain the difference between an unsecured creditor and a secured creditor.

Problem 1.2

➢ In what way is an unsecured creditor disadvantaged compared with a creditor who has a security interest?

---

2. In Georgia, the residential lender has a security deed not a mortgage.

3. In the revised version of Article 1 of the Uniform Commercial Code the definition of security interest is contained in § 1-203 ("Lease Distinguished from a Security Interest").

➤ What is the difference between recourse and non-recourse financing?

Problem 1.3

➤ What must an unsecured creditor do in order to assert an interest in personal property in which the debtor has a transferable interest?

2. Laws Limiting Debt Collection Efforts

There are a number of consumer protection laws that may affect the ability of creditors including secured creditors to collect on debts. These include, for example, the Fair Debt Collections Practice Act, 15 U.S.C § 1692 et seq., which has been amended by the Consumer Financial Protection Act of 2010. The act limits the actions of collection agents in their efforts to collect debts from consumers.

The Bankruptcy Code,[4] § 362, provides for an Automatic Stay preventing creditors from continuing collection efforts against debtors including the issuance of process, the continuation of any judicial or administrative proceeding, arbitration, civil actions generally, and any attempt to take possession of property of the bankruptcy estate (generally, property of the debtor as of the date of filing the bankruptcy petition). An exception, among others, provides for allowing certain creditors with a grace period to file a financing statement perfecting their security interest even after the bankruptcy petition is filed. *See,* Bankruptcy Code § 363(b)(3).

B. Creation of a Financial Obligation

U.C.C. Article 9 is about using personal property as collateral for a financial obligation, that is, in order to create a *Security Interest. See,* §§ 9-109(a), "Scope" of Article 9 and 1-201(37).

The financial obligation created might be an instrument as defined in U.C.C. Article 3 (negotiable promissory notes or perhaps drafts including checks) or a contractual obligation such as a contract setting forth a schedule of payments. Note that pursuant to § 2-210(4), a prohibition on the assignment of the performance under a contract does not act as a prohibition on the assignment of a financial obligation.

---

4. The Bankruptcy Code is Title 11 of the United States Code. The current version of the Bankruptcy Code was amended by the Bankruptcy Abuse Prevention and Consumer Protection Act (BAPCPA) enacted in 2005.

Questions

Problem 1.4

➤ Why would a lender want collateral?

Problem 1.5

➤ If a potential borrower does not have collateral, how might that lender attempt to ensure payment of a financial obligation?

Example and Questions

Lynch buys a fishing boat for $3,000 from a Boat Dealer. In exchange, Lynch gives the Boat Dealer a check for the $3,000, which subsequently bounces.

Questions

Problem 1.6

➤ Under U.C.C. Article 2, has there been a sale? Explain.

Problem 1.7

➤ Does the Boat Dealer have a security interest in the boat?

Problem 1.8

➤ What if Lynch sells the boat to Dag for $2,000 cash even though he never paid for the boat?

➤ Who ultimately gets the boat, Dag or the Boat Dealer? Explain.

Example and Questions

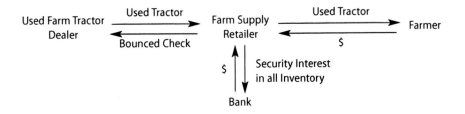

Farm Supply Retailer borrows money from the Bank to buy inventory. To collateralize the loan, evidenced by a promissory note, the Farm Supply Company signs a Security Agreement granting to the Bank a Security Interest in inventory.

Used Farm Tractor Dealer sells a used tractor to Farm Supply Retailer who pays for it with a bounced check. Meanwhile, Farm Supply Retailer sells the used tractor to Farmer for cash, who then takes possession.

Questions

Problem 1.9

➤ Upon the sale of the used tractor from Used Farm Tractor Dealer to Farm Supply Retailer, what interest does the Retailer have?

➤ What is the Retailer's status?

Problem 1.10

➤ When the check bounces, what options does the Used Farm Tractor Dealer have against the Farm Supply Retailer?

Problem 1.11

➤ Once the Farm Supply Retailer obtained possession of the used tractor, does the Bank have any interest in that particular tractor?

Problem 1.12

➤ Once the used tractor is sold to the Farmer, does the Used Farm Tractor Dealer have any rights against the Farmer? Explain.

Problem 1.13

➤ Once Farmer pays for the tractor which party, the Used Farm Tractor Dealer or the Bank, has first claim to the cash from the sale?

➤ Does either party, the Used Farm Tractor Dealer or the Bank, still have any rights in the tractor?

C. Classification of Collateral

A *Collateral Index* that classifies the various types of personal property is set-forth in **Appendix B** of this book. Review that index and list each collateral type under one of the following headings:

a.   *Tangibles*: collateral with physical form.

b. *Quasi-tangibles or quasi-intangibles*: collateral that embody (reify) legal rights in physical form.

c. *Intangibles*: rights in collateral which have no physical form, but which serve as evidence of something else.

Note that collateral types that do not easily fit any of the above categories such as letter-of-credit rights, electronic chattel paper, and money (deposit accounts) have special rules regarding their use as collateral.

Questions

Problem 1.14

➤ What are fixtures? *See*, U.C.C. §9-102(a)(41).

Problem 1.15

➤ How are trade fixtures classified?

Morgan County Feeders, Inc. v. McCormick

836 P.2d 1051 (Ct. App. Co. Div. III, 1992)
(edited opinion with Code references updated within brackets)
ROTHEMBERG, J.

In 1990, Morgan County Feeders, as a secured creditor, obtained a default judgment against Neil Allen for $1,461,019. Morgan County Feeders attempted to garnish 45 longhorn cows and one bull that were in the possession of Roy Creamer. Creamer contested the garnishment, and Morgan County Feeders filed a post-judgment motion for issuance of a writ of garnishment and to join third persons who also claimed an interest in the cattle. The court granted Morgan County Feeders' motion. The parties then stipulated to the sale of the cattle, and the proceeds were placed in the registry of the court pending a hearing.

At the hearing, Morgan County Feeders claimed a priority in the proceeds based on its perfected security interest arising from a security agreement with Allen, which, in part, contained an after-acquired property clause. McCormick claimed an interest in the proceeds based on an oral agreement with Allen to buy the cattle.

After making extensive findings of fact and conclusions of law, the trial court entered judgment in favor of Morgan County Feeders, finding that the 45-longhorn cattle were "equipment" and not "inventory" under the Uniform Commercial Code and that Allen had no authority to dispose of the longhorn cattle free of Morgan County Feeders' perfected security interest. Accordingly, the court awarded Morgan County Feeders the sale proceeds minus certain costs owed to Creamer. McCormick is the only party that has appealed the judgment.

I.

McCormick first contends that the trial court erred in determining that the cattle purchased by Allen were equipment, rather than inventory. We disagree.

Under the Uniform Commercial Code, "goods" are defined as, "all things which are moveable at the time the security interest attaches...." §9-102(a)(44). Goods are classified under four major types, which are mutually exclusive. These include: consumer goods [§9-102(23)]; equipment [§9-102(33)]; farm products [§9-102(34)]; and inventory [§9-102(48)].

Here, the parties agree that the cattle constitute "goods" under the Uniform Commercial Code. They further agree that the cattle are not "farm products." Thus, the remaining issue surrounding the cattle is whether they should be designated as inventory or equipment. The distinction is important because buyers of inventory in the ordinary course of business take free of perfected security interests.

Section 9-102(33), provides that goods are equipment:

> if they are used or bought for use primarily in business (including farming or a profession) ... or if the goods are not included in the definitions of inventory, farm products, or consumer goods. [previous definition under superseded §9-109(2) but still explanatory]

In contrast, §9-109(4) provides that goods are inventory:

> if they are held by a person who holds them for sale or lease or to be furnished under contracts of service or if he has so furnished them, or if they are ... materials used or consumed in a business. Inventory of a person is not to be classified as his equipment. [previous definition under superseded §9-109(4)] [*See*, current definition in §9-102(49)].

In ascertaining whether goods are inventory or equipment, the principal use of the property is determinative. The factors to be considered in determining principal use include whether the goods are for immediate or ultimate sale and whether they have a relatively long or short period of use in the business.

Goods used in a business are equipment when they are fixed assets or have, as identifiable units, a relatively long period of use. They are inventory, even though not held for sale, if they are used up or consumed in a short period of time in the production of some end product.

The classification of "goods" under §4-9-109 is a question of fact, and therefore, the trial court's classification must be upheld if there is support in the record for that determination.

At trial, the court determined that the longhorn cattle were "equipment" and not "inventory" because:

> Allen did not acquire or hold them for the principal purpose of immediate or ultimate sale or lease.... Instead, the cattle were to be used principally for recreational cattle drives.... While Allen might have occasionally leased the cattle to other entrepreneurs, it was his intention to utilize the cattle principally in his own recreational business....

Thus, the court concluded that McCormick bought the cattle subject to Morgan County Feeders' security interest.

Although we recognize that the classification of cattle as "equipment," rather than "inventory," is highly unusual, we also recognize that the evidence presented to the trial court disclosed unusual circumstances, and we conclude that the record supports the court's classification.

Allen testified that his purpose for purchasing the longhorn cows was to use them on cattle drives and that these cows have a relatively long period of use in comparison to rodeo calves and feeder cattle. Several other witnesses also testified that Allen had stated his intent to use the longhorn cows for recreational cattle drives. Thus, the trial court was justified in rejecting McCormick's contention that the cattle were purchased only for rodeos. And, it did not err in finding that, under these unique circumstances; the cattle should be classified as "equipment."

In light of this conclusion, we need not address McCormick's additional contention that the trial court erred in finding that McCormick was not a buyer in the ordinary course of business.

II.

McCormick next contends that Morgan County Feeders authorized the sale of the 45-longhorn cows, and thereby waived its security interest in them, by allowing Allen to purchase them from his own checking account without remitting the proceeds to Morgan County Feeders. We disagree.

Section 4-9-306(2), C.R.S. provides:

> Except where this article otherwise provides, a security interest continues in collateral notwithstanding sale, exchange, or other disposition thereof *unless the disposition was authorized by the secured party in the security agreement or otherwise,* and also continues in any iden-

tifiable proceeds including collections received by the debtor. (emphasis added). [succeeded by 9-315].

The security agreement between Allen and Morgan County Feeders provided:

> Cattle shall be released from Secured Party's security interest from time-to-time in conjunction with the sale of such cattle provided that Secured Party receives concurrently with such release, an amount equal to the entire net proceeds to Debtor from such sale until the entire outstanding principal balance of the Loans and all accrued interest is due and payable in full.
>
> ...
>
> Debtor shall be in default under this Agreement upon the happening of any of the following events or conditions (Events of Default):
>
> ...
>
> > (e) the sale, lease, assignment, transfer or other disposition of a substantial amount of the assets of the Debtor except for cattle disposed of in the ordinary course of business ...
> > (f) ... sale or encumbrance of the Cattle (except as specifically allowed herein)....

Here, it is uncontroverted that Morgan County Feeders did not give written consent for the sale of the cattle to McCormick. Thus, any authorization must be implied from the conduct of the parties. We conclude there is record support for the trial court's conclusion that Morgan County Feeders did not impliedly waive its security interest.

* * *

Questions

Problem 1.16

➤ When the Cattle were sold by stipulation of the parties, what happened to their asserted security interests? *See,* § 9-102(a)(64), "Proceeds."

Problem 1.17

➤ Why were the Cattle not classified as "farm products"? *See* § 9-102(34), (35).

Problem 1.18

➤ Why did the Court hold that McCormick, no doubt buying in good faith, bought the cattle subject to Morgan County Feeders' security interest? *See* § 9-315(a)(1).

Problem 1.19

➤ Was McCormick a BIOC? Explain.

Problem 1.20

➤ What arguments may have McCormick advanced to support a contention that Morgan County Feeders waived its security interest not
withstanding the language of the Agreement between Allan and Morgan County Feeders?

Problem 1.21

➤ If like Billy Crystal in "City Slickers," one of the "Dudes" on the cattle
drive had taken a calf home with him for a pet, how would that calf
be classified?

Problem 1.22

➤ Would Morgan County Feeders security interest follow the calf, making the Dude potentially liable to Morgan County Feeders as the secured party? *See* §§ 9-315(a)(1), 2-403(2)(3), "Entrusting," 9-315
Comment 2, 9-320(e) Comment 4.

Example and Questions

Law Student, still having funds after paying tuition, decides to buy a new
car. He goes to the local Jeep Dealer and picks out a new Grand Cherokee cost-
ing, after negotiations, $42,000. Dealer presents Student with a contract valu-
ing Student's trade-in at $7,000 with a balance due of $35,000 plus tax, tag,
and title. Dealer requires full payment on or before delivery. Student wishes to
finance the balance at an attractive 2.9% interest rate offered by Chrysler Financial. Dealer arranges the Financing. The transaction looks like this:

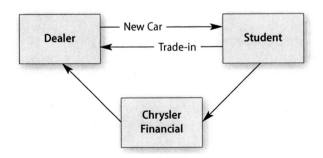

Questions

Problem 1.23

➤ What does the Student give to Chrysler Financial?

Problem 1.24

➤ What does Chrysler Financial give to Dealer?

Problem 1.25

➤ What is Chrysler Financial's business?

Problem 1.26

➤ What did the Dealer get for the new car?

Problem 1.27

➤ How does the definition of "value" for Article 2 purposes differ from the definition of value for Article 3 purposes?

Problem 1.28

➤ What interest does Chrysler Financial have in the new car?

➤ Does that interest make Chrysler Financial a purchaser? Explain.

Problem 1.29

➤ What interest does Student have in the new car?

Problem 1.30

➤ What does Chrysler Financial do to indicate it has an interest in the car? *See,* §9-311(a)(2) and (3), and O.C.G.A. Title 40, Chapter 3.

Problem 1.31

➤ What is Chrysler Financial's purpose in indicating it has an interest in the car?

Example and Questions

Chrysler Financial finances many thousands of automobile sales. Chrysler, LLC, the manufacturing entity insists on full payment for its car at the factory door. Without going into more detail yet, Chrysler Financial is going to need immediate cash in order to finance the buyers of automobiles who insist on and need credit extending from three to six years.

Questions

Problem 1.32

➤ What collateral does Chrysler Financial have when it borrows money from wholesale lenders (a group of large commercial banks)? See the chart below.

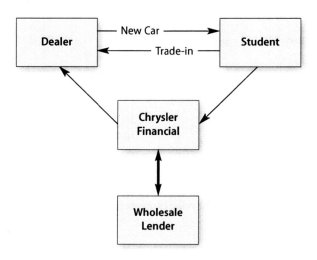

Problem 1.33

➤ What collateral does Chrysler Financial assign to the Wholesale Lenders (a group of commercial banks)?

Problem 1.34

➤ What is Chrysler Financial's[5] role once the above-diagramed transaction is completed?

5. Ally Financial finances automobile purchases for Chrysler and General Motors.

Chapter Two

Scope—U.C.C. §9-109

A. Scope of §9-109

The security interest in the collateral is created by contract.

In re Topgallant Lines, Inc.

154 B.R. 368 (Bankr. S.D. Ga. 1993)
(affirmed 20 F.3d 1175, 11th Cir. 1994) (edited opinion; U.C.C.
references updated; and bracketed material added)
NANGLE, District Judge

Ambassador Factors the appellee/cross-appellant, appeals the February 4, 1991, decision of the bankruptcy court which granted appellants' Motion for Summary Judgment on the ground that valid maritime liens are superior to perfected Uniform Commercial Code (U.C.C.) security interests in the same collateral.

* * *

On April 19, 1989, the Debtor and Ambassador Factors (Ambassador) entered into a security agreement covering personal property, accounts receivable, inventory, and equipment of the Debtor. On April 28, 1989, Ambassador recorded two Uniform Commercial Code Financing Statements in the Office of the Clerk of Superior Court of Chatham County, Georgia, covering "[a]ll present and hereafter created and/or acquired accounts receivable, inventory, machinery and equipment and general intangibles [of the debtor] ..." On August 30, 1989, Ambassador filed a similar U.C.C. financing statement with the Secretary of State of New Jersey.

On December 13, 1989, the Debtor filed its voluntary petition under Chapter 11 of the bankruptcy code in the United States Bankruptcy Court for the Southern District of Georgia.

* * *

FABC, [First American Bulk Carrier Corporation,] and other creditors have filed proofs of claim in the bankruptcy court asserting that their claims are, in whole or in part, secured by maritime liens on the Debtor's freights, including those freights held in the sequestered account. Ambassador disputes the lien status and priority of these claims, and alleges that its perfected U.C.C. security interest takes priority over the interests of the maritime liens claimants.

* * *

[Article 9 applies generally to commercial financing security, hence, it covers certain transactions that might be otherwise considered sales, consignments, conditional sales contracts (like title retention contracts, *see* §2-401(1)) or security interests disguised as leases. *See*, §1-201(37).]

DISCUSSION

* * *

Ambassador contests the bankruptcy court's holding that " ... valid maritime liens as hereafter allowed will be afforded priority over perfected U.C.C. security interests ..." *Topgallant I,* 125 B.R. at 687. In reaching this conclusion, the bankruptcy court first held that the Federal Maritime Lien Act, 46 U.S.C. §31301 *et seq.*, does not specifically supersede the U.C.C. *Id.* at 685. The priority provisions of the U.C.C., however, have no effect on the maritime liens created under the Act since O.C.G.A. §11-9-109(c)(1) makes the U.C.C. inapplicable to a security interest subject to any statute of the United States. *Id.* at 686. Alternatively, the bankruptcy court found that the U.C.C. applies only to consensual transactions, while "the claim of maritime lien holders, by definition, is not consensual." *Id.*

Ambassador contends that the creation and validity of maritime liens are excluded from the U.C.C., but that priority issues involving maritime liens are governed by the U.C.C.

* * *

Ambassador advances that since freights arise from the performance of services under a contract or affreightment and charter hire includes freights arising from performance of a charter, freights and subfreights fall within the definition of accounts contained in O.C.G.A. §11-9-102(a)(2).

[However], §11-9-109(c)(1) renders the maritime liens of the claimants outside the ambit of Article 9.

* * *

[A.] *The U.C.C. applies only to consensual transactions, and maritime liens, by definition, are not consensual.*

* * *

The Maritime Lien Act automatically gives rise to a maritime lien when a person furnishes necessaries to a vessel, and neither intent nor consent is involved in its formation. 46 U.S.C. §31342(a)(1). *See also* Gilmore & Black, 586–589 (2d ed. 1975) ("… [M]aritime liens have extraordinarily little in common with land liens, including consensual security interests."). Since maritime liens do not fall within Article Nine's scope, the priority provisions of the U.C.C. are inapplicable.

* * *

[B.] *Maritime lienors have priority over holders of U.C.C. security interests.*

Having determined that the priority provisions of the U.C.C. do not apply to maritime liens, this Court must decide whether valid maritime liens have priority over a perfected U.C.C. security interest. Case law, whether pre- or post-U.C.C., compels an affirmative response.

"Any priority given by the statute of a state, or by decisions at common law or in equity, is immaterial … the admiralty court of the United States, enforcing the lien because it is maritime in nature … must give it the rank to which it is entitled by the principles of maritime and admiralty law." *The J.E. RUMBELL,* 148 U.S. 1, 19, 13 S.Ct. 498, 503, 37 L.Ed. 345 (1893). Maritime liens prevail over non-maritime claims. *Taiwan Int'l Line, Ltd. v. Matthew Ship Chartering Ltd.,* 546 F.Supp. 826 (S.D.N.Y.1982). Although few cases have dealt specifically with clashes between the U.C.C. and maritime law, those decisions that have addressed the issue resolve any conflict in favor of maritime law. *See, e.g., Pacific Caribbean,* 789 F.2d at 1408 (Maritime lienor not required to perfect interest under Article Nine to prevail over bankruptcy trustee); *Matthews v. Richmond,* 11 Wash.App. 703, 525 P.2d 810 (1974) (Plaintiff's perfection of a security interest in the vessel did not establish his priority over a subsequent maritime lienor). Thus, Ambassador's perfected U.C.C. security interest is subordinate to valid maritime liens....

* * *

Questions

Problem 2.1

➢ What are the two primary reasons why Article 9 does not apply in this case?

Problem 2.2

➤ What is the significance of "priority"?

Problem 2.3

➤ Once a bankruptcy is filed, the trustee (whether or not one is actually appointed) has the status of a judicial lien creditor under state law for the benefit of the bankruptcy estate. *See*, Bankruptcy Code §544. How does this affect the priority of claims?

Problem 2.4

➤ How is security interest defined for Article 9 purposes?

Problem 2.5

➤ Section 9-109, the "scope" provision includes an agricultural lien. For what purpose is it included?

Agricultural liens mean an interest in farm products that include livestock (born or unborn). A financing statement must be filed to perfect all agricultural liens. Additionally, a purchaser cannot take farm products free of a security interest when purchasing the products from a person engaged in farming operations. *See*, §§9-102(5), 9-109, 9-308, 9-310.

Liens as defined by Article 9 arise involuntarily when personal or real property is subject to a monetary obligation that arises through a judicial order or by statute. Liens are not covered by Article 9, but are discussed within the scope of prioritization of claims against a debtor. Types of liens can include: (1) statutory liens, such as, (a) common law liens including construction, artesian, and mechanics liens, (b) federal tax liens, (c) hospital liens, and (d) property tax liens; (2) security interest referred to as liens; and (3) judicial liens. See Bankruptcy Code §507 to understand the order of distribution of funds to unsecured creditors. This is generally referred to as the *waterfall of priority*. Do not confuse the use of the term priority under the bankruptcy code with its use in Article 9 of the U.C.C. Bankruptcy Code §507 establishes a priority of distribution from the bankruptcy estate for unsecured creditors.

When purchasing a home, the Buyers either sign a security deed, used within Georgia, or a mortgage and promissory note in favor of the lending bank. Note that the security deed leaves the title with the bank, whereas, the mortgage leaves title with the individual homebuyers. Real estate law not Article 9 covers both mortgages and security deeds.

Questions

Problem 2.6

➤ Joe borrows $100,000 from Loan Originator, securing his repayment obligations, evidenced by a promissory note (an instrument under U.C.C. Article 3) by granting the Loan Originator a mortgage on his land. Does Article 9 apply to the creation of a real estate mortgage?

Problem 2.7

➤ What if Loan Originator negotiates, that is, sells, along with notes arising from other real estate mortgages, the promissory note to a Bank?

➤ Is this transaction subject to Article 9?

Problem 2.8

➤ Do the mortgages still serve as collateral for the repayment of the notes? *See*, §9-308(e).

B. Article 9 Coverage—§9-109

Article 9 covers commercial financing collateral, that is, any personal property likely used as collateral by an entity in the business of "selling money" to secure payment of a monetary obligation. It also covers collateralized credit sales. By definition anyone getting such an interest in property is a purchaser. *See*, §1-201(32, 33).

With only minimal exceptions (generally in the Consumer sale context), Article 9 requires a secured creditor, that is, an entity supplying money or financing an entity through a credit extension or by making loans, to do something (perfect) to alert (give notice to) third parties dealing with the Debtor that the Debtor's property *may* be encumbered, that is, that the debtor may have less than clean title or even that title to the collateral lies elsewhere. *See*, §9-202, "Title of Collateral Immaterial."

Third parties are parties other than the Obligor or the Debtor who granted the security interest and the Secured Party who is generally in a first priority position by virtue of the general rule that first to perfect is first in right. Note there are exceptions arising from non-U.C.C. statutes and even under the U.C.C. itself. *See*, e.g. §9-324, "Priority of Purchase—Money Security Interest."

A secured creditor perfects by filing, notation on a certificate of title (over the road vehicles), control, possession (of pawnshop, for example), or automatically upon attachment of the security interest (for example, the sale by a merchant on credit from inventory of a good that becomes a consumer good, such as a refrigerator where the Debtor (BIOC) has signed a Security Agreement). Note this is a one-shot sale not really a commercial financing arrangement, although the installment contract or note generated by the Debtor may be used as collateral.

Manufacturers, wholesalers, and retailers need cash to operate. Manufacturers generally insist on cash before releasing goods to the wholesaler or retailers. Wholesalers and retailers may take cash or sell on credit to Buyers. Buyers need to have a source of cash. Suppliers of cash, whether used for purchasing goods for resale or operating expenses generally insist on collateral. Collateral may be tangible (goods in inventory), quasi-tangible (paper that embodies title to goods like negotiable instruments), or intangible (accounts, contract rights, and other promises wherein the paper is merely evidence of the debt).

This is not to claim that secured lending is the only way to finance a business. In fact, much short term lending to established businesses is unsecured. The issuance of common and preferred stocks is another way for a business to raise funds, which like unsecured credit does not involve an Article 9 transaction.

Questions

Problem 2.9

➤ Perfection of tangible collateral is generally by filing or possession. Explain.

Problem 2.10

➤ Perfection of a quasi-tangible is best by control or possession. Explain.

Problem 2.11

➤ Perfection of intangibles is by filing. Why?

Problem 2.12

➤ The litigation involving Article 9 is generally about whether a secured party is perfected, and if perfected, what collateral is covered and what is the secured party's priority. Generally, first to perfect is first in priority, but there are exceptions. Consider, near-cash like negotiable instruments (checks and negotiable promissory notes), investment securities, or negotiable documents of title.

➤ Now, compare all of those that are sold or assigned for purposes of financing with accounts receivables. What additional factors must you consider when account receivables are used as collateral?

Problem 2.13

➤ There are exclusions from Article 9 to the extent that other law governs. In what way might Article 9 apply to the listed exclusions in §9-109(c)?

Problem 2.14

➤ Exclusions based on non-code law are found in §9-109(d). How does this section's exclusions differ from those in §9-109(c)?

➤ Exclusions in sections 9-109(d)(4), (5), (6), and (7) have something in common. In other words, what is the reason for the exclusions?

Problem 2.15

➤ Assuming a secured creditor does not perfect, may such creditor still enforce such interest against the debtor?

Problem 2.16

➤ May a Debtor use stock certificates as collateral?

➤ If so, does it matter who possesses the actual certificates?

C. Distinguishing a Lease from a Security Agreement

Distinguishing a true lease from a security interest called a lease may be crucial. The Article 9 Scope section, 9-109, indicates that Article 9 "applies to: (1) a transaction, regardless of form, that creates a security interest in personal property...." This excludes true leases which are covered by U.C.C. Article 2A.

Questions

Problem 2.17

➤ What is it specifically that the financier of a true lease does not have to do that a financier of a security interest disguised as a lease is well advised to do?

Problem 2.18

➤ Why is that important?

Pursuant to §1-201(37),[1] a transaction called a lease is really a disguised security agreement if:

---

1. In the revised (2006) Article 1, the pertinent section is 1-203.

(1) the lease is not subject to termination by the lessee during its term, and

    (a) the original term of the lease is equal to or greater than the remaining economic life of the goods,

    (b) the lessee is bound to renew the lease for the remaining economic life of the goods or is bound to become the owner of the goods,

    (c) the lessee has an option to renew the lease for the remaining economic life of the goods for no additional consideration or nominal additional consideration upon compliance with the lease agreement, or

    (d) the lessee has an option to become the owner of the goods for no additional consideration or nominal additional consideration upon compliance with the lease agreement.

Note all of the above implicate economic decision-making. In other words if the lessee has really paid for the goods, for example, as illustrated by sub-sections (a) and (b), or it makes no economic sense for the lessee not to exercise the option to buy based upon the original lease contract, the agreement really creates a sale subject to a security interest.

Example and Questions

Instead of buying a car, Law Student decides to lease a car through the law firm she is about to join. Of course, since the vehicle is now a business expense, therefore tax write-off, Law Student, soon to be Law Graduate, decides on a Mercedes S-Class.

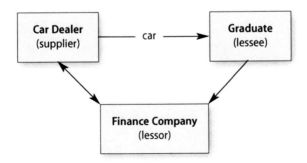

Questions

Problem 2.19

➤ What does the Finance Company get from the Lessee?

Problem 2.20

➤ What does the Finance Company give the Supplier?

Problem 2.21

➤ What does the Supplier give the Finance Company?

Problem 2.22

➤ Which party, Lessor or Graduate, gets the benefit of Article 2A contract warranties?

Problem 2.23

➤ If the Lessee assumes risk of loss of the goods and is responsible for all fees and expenses for the use of the goods, does this convert the lease agreement into a security interest?

In re Lash

2010 WL 5141760 (Bankr. M.D. N.C. 2010)
(edited; most citations omitted; added text in brackets)
WALDREP, United States Bankruptcy Judge

[Note: This is a bankruptcy matter and the adverse parties are the Chapter 13 Debtor, although it may often be the Standing Chapter 13 Bankruptcy Trustee, and Tucker Capital, claiming rights as Lessor under a true lease.]

MEMORANDUM OPINION

On or about May 24, 2007, the Debtor, as Lessee, and Tucker Capital, as Lessor, entered into an agreement titled Equipment Lease (the "Agreement") for the use of a 2003 Freightliner.

The Agreement provides ... [in addition to periodic lease payments] that:

> Lessee or Lessor may terminate the Lease at the expiration of the Initial Term by giving the other at least 90 days prior written notice of termination. If neither Lessee nor Lessor gives such notice, then the term of this Lease shall be extended automatically on the same rental and other terms set forth herein ... for successive periods of one month (each, an "Extension Term") until terminated by either Lessee or Lessor after giving the other party at least 90 days prior written notice of termination.

Paragraph 13 of the Agreement, entitled "Loss or Damage," provides that if the equipment is "lost, stolen, destroyed, damaged beyond repair, or rendered permanently unfit for use for any reason," then the Debtor will pay Tucker Capital all remaining rent for the Initial Term, as well as the TRAC [Terminal Rental Adjustment Clause] Amount. Tucker Capital would then transfer all of its rights and interests in the equipment to the Debtor. Paragraph 13 further provides that "[a]ny insurance or condemnation proceeds received shall be credited to Lessee's obligation under [Paragraph 13] and Lessor shall be entitled to any surplus." Pursuant to Paragraph 14, the Debtor is required to obtain insurance on the Freightliner.

* * *

DISCUSSION

State law governs property rights, including the existence, validity and extent of a security interest. *Butner v. U.S.*, 440 U.S. 48, 54–55 (1979). Thus, state law determines whether an agreement creates a true lease or a security interest. *Powers v. Royce, Inc. (In re Powers)*, 983 F.2d 88, 90 (7th Cir.1993).

* * *

A.   *The Bright Line Test*

Under [the] U.C.C., whether an agreement creates a true lease or a security interest is governed by a two-part test. The first step is frequently referred to as the bright-line test. To satisfy the bright-line test, which is codified in U.C.C. §1-203(b) [Revised Article 1], [§1-201(37) in Georgia], the court must determine that the "lease" is not subject to termination by the lessee and that at least one of four enumerated conditions is satisfied. They are whether the transaction in the form of a lease creates a security interest [when] the consideration that the lessee is to pay the lessor for the right to possession and use of the goods is an obligation for the term of the lease and is not subject to termination by the lessee, and:

(1)   The original term of the lease is equal to or greater than the remaining economic life of the goods;

(2)   The lessee is bound to renew the lease for the remaining economic life of the goods or is bound to become the owner of the goods;

(3)   The lessee has an option to renew the lease for the remaining economic life of the goods for no additional consideration or for nominal additional consideration upon compliance with the lease agreement; or

(4)   The lessee has an option to become the owner of the goods for no additional consideration or for nominal additional consideration upon compliance with the lease agreement.

"[A]ll of these tests focus on economics, not the intent of the parties." (Comment 37 to §1-201) [Whether an agreement is a true lease or a security interest disguised as a lease is a matter of law.]

* * *

In this case, the Debtor, as Lessee, is not permitted to terminate the Agreement until the expiration of the Initial Term, so the first part of the bright-line test has been satisfied. However, the second part of the test has not been satisfied. No evidence was presented regarding the value of the Freightliner. The Plan assigned the claim a secured value of $18,500.00, and Schedule D assigned the Freightliner a secured value of $20,000.00. However, neither of these sources is, without a proper foundation, admissible as evidence of value. Fed.R.Evid. 201; *see also In re Harmony Holdings, LLC,* 393 B.R. 409, 413 (Bankr.D.S.C.2008) (noting that while a bankruptcy court may take judicial notice of the content of bankruptcy schedules, facts contained within such pleadings must comply with the Federal Rules of Evidence). At the hearing, although the Debtor and Tucker Capital argued about whether the TRAC Amount is a nominal payment, neither party presented any evidence regarding the value of the Freightliner. Thus, it is impossible for the Court to determine whether the TRAC Amount is a nominal payment since there is no evidence regarding either the present value of the collateral, or even what the parties initially projected the value of the collateral to be at the end of the lease term. Therefore, the Court must move past the bright-line test and consider the economic realities of the transaction.

B.   *The Economic Realities Test*

If the bright-line test is not satisfied, "then a security interest will not be conclusively found to exist, and the court will need to consider other factors." As one court colorfully put it:

> Failure to meet one of these conditions means only that the document is not conclusively a security agreement; the pinball has safely rolled past four holes each marked security agreement. Evasion of these four holes does not earn one enough points to become a lessee. Finding economic life beyond the lease term and seeing no nominal consideration option, what should a court do? The court must then answer whether the lessor retained a reversionary interest. If there is a meaningful reversionary interest—either an up-side right or a down-side risk—the parties have signed a lease, not a security agreement. If there is no reversionary interest, the parties have signed a security interest, not a lease.

Sankey v. ABCO Leasing (In re Sankey), 307 B.R. 674, 680 (D.Alaska 2004).

A determination that a lessor has retained a meaningful reversionary interest typically derives from the following facts: "(1) at the outset of the lease the parties expect the goods to retain some significant residual value at the end of the lease term; and (2) the lessor retains some entrepreneurial stake (either the possibility of gain or the risk of loss) in the value of the goods at the end of the lease term." 319 B.R. at 715. When a purchase option is involved, if the lessee's only economically sensible option is to exercise the option, then the agreement will be considered to create a security interest.

[One court found:]

> The economic substance of the TRAC Lease is no different from a typical installment loan in which the lender has agreed to a balloon payment in lieu of a down payment. Whether characterized as a lease, which uses terms such as "Estimated Residual Value" as a substitute for "balloon" and "rental payments" instead of "installment payments," or characterized as an installment loan, the economic characteristics are identical and can be generically described as follows: The borrower finances the acquisition of equipment through a loan from a finance company. The loan is repaid over a set term, at the end of which the borrower must make the balloon payment. The "collateral" for the financing is sold at the end of the loan term, and the proceeds are applied toward the borrower's balloon payment. If there is a deficiency, the borrower is responsible for paying it. If there is a surplus, the borrower retains it. The lender has no expectation or right to retain ownership of the "collateral" at the conclusion of the loan period.

* * *

An examination of the Agreement, which was admitted into evidence, reveals that Tucker Capital has retained no meaningful reversionary interest in the collateral. The TRAC provision provides that the equipment "will be sold" at the expiration of the Initial Term of the Agreement. Thus, the Debtor is required to comply with this provision, and does not have any alternative, as Tucker Capital contends. After the sale, the Debtor is liable for any deficiency and entitled to any surplus. Therefore, Tucker Capital bears no risk of loss, and cannot receive any benefit if the Freightliner appreciates in value. Regardless of whether the Freightliner is worth $1,000,000.00 or $1.00 at the end of the lease term, Tucker Capital is entitled to receive the TRAC Amount of $4,225.00—no more and no less. By comparison, the Debtor bears all the risk if the Freightliner depreciates and reaps all the reward if it appreciates. If the value is $1.00, the Debtor must pay Tucker Capital $4,225.00, plus any costs of sale. If the value is $1,000,000.00, the Debtor is entitled to receive that amount, less the TRAC Amount and any costs of sale. The TRAC clause, as was the case with the nearly identical provision in the *Grubbs* case, removes any meaningful reversionary interest from Tucker Capital and places it with the Debtor. Therefore, even with no evidence regarding the value of the Freightliner, it is clear that under the facts of this case, the Agreement created a security interest, not a lease.

* * *

Questions

Problem 2.24

➢ What is the difference between a TRAC clause and a Residual Payment Clause? (*See* the following questions.)

Problem 2.25

➢ Why, particularly in bankruptcy cases, is it so important to determine if a lease is a true lease or a security interest disguised as a lease?

Problem 2.26

➢ What if the Lessee had the option to buy the truck for its fair market value at the end of the lease term?

Problem 2.27

➢ What if at the end of a lease term, the leased equipment is sold for less than the Estimated Residual Value obligating the Lessee to make up the difference under a TRAC clause?

Problem 2.28

➢ Does §9-611(b) require a lessor to give notice to a Lessee of a sale of a leased good after a default and the surrender of these goods to the Lessor? Explain. *See, Aniebue v. Jaguar Credit Corp.*, 708 S.E. 2d 4 (Ga. App. 2011).

D. True Leases

The following examples and questions are based on In re EQUITABLE FINANCIAL MANAGEMENT, INC., 164 B.R. 53 (Bankr. W.D. Pa. 1994). Assume this transaction is a true lease. Note that in this case, the Lessor was a Debtor under the bankruptcy code. The trustee was attempting to claim that CPI was unsecured.

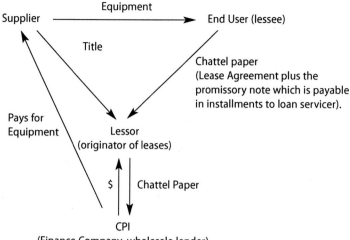

Explanation

In a finance lease, §2A-103(1)(g), the End User (the lessee) selects the goods.

The End User executes a lease agreement with the Lessor and agrees to sign a monetary obligation at an appropriate time.

The Finance Company, CPI, contracts with the Lessor to purchase the equipment from the Supplier chosen by the Lessee.

The equipment is delivered to the Lessee, who then signs a Certificate of Delivery and Acceptance triggering the Lessor's obligation to pay the Supplier. The Lessor borrows the money from the Finance Company who may or may not file an Article 9 Financing Statement covering the equipment. Note title is with the Lessor, hence, filing if done, would be in the Lessor's name or as precautionary matter in the End User's name since a court may well decide that the transaction is a security agreement disguised as a lease.

Questions

Problem 2.29

➢ What is the collateral?

The chattel paper is then assigned by the Lessor to the Finance Company which can take a security interest in such paper either by filing or possession (the preferred method).

Problem 2.30

➤ What constitutes chattel paper?

In exchange the Finance Company pays the Lessor a sum representing the present value (§2A-103(1)(u)) of the stream of interest payments due from the End User to the Lessor minus a discount on the Contract price paid for the equipment effectively giving the Finance Company a higher interest rate than is set forth in the Lease Agreement.

Note that the Lessor is not in the business of selling goods. Warranty obligations go from the Supplier (analogous to an Article 2 Seller) to the Lessee (analogous to an Article 2 Buyer). *See,* §§2A-209 through 2A-216. Georgia adopted the alternative A to §2A-216 (third party beneficiaries of warranties).

Problem 2.31

➤ Why would a Lessor file a financing statement as if the End User is an Article 9 debtor?

E. Car Leasing: An Example of an Operating Lease

Capitalized Cost: Often called the *cap cost,* this is basically the *negotiated* price of the car and all the options. This becomes one of several figures used in calculating a monthly lease payment.

Net Cap Cost: The Gross Cap Cost (selling price you negotiate with the dealer) *plus* add-on-fees and taxes, and any prior loan balances, *minus* any Cap Cost Reductions (down payments, trade-in, or rebates).

Money Factor: Also called a *lease factor* or even a *lease fee.* This is the interest rate you are being charged. It is expressed as a multiplier that can be used to calculate your monthly payments. For example, 7.2 percent interest, when expressed as a money factor is 0.0033. A money factor can be converted to an interest rate multiplying the number by 24. An interest rate can be converted to a money factor by dividing the number by 24. (Always use 24 regardless of the loan length). [The reason for the use of 24 is beyond the needs of this course].

Depreciation Fee: The portion of your payment that pays the leasing company for the loss in value of its car, spread over the term of the lease, based on the miles you intend to drive and the time you intend to keep the car. You pay an equal portion of the total expected depreciation each month. This is calculated as follows:

Depreciation Fee = (Net Cap Cost−Residual) / Term

Monthly Lease Payment: This combines the depreciation fee, finance fee and the sales tax. Lease Payment is calculated as follows:

Let's assume you have decided on a 3 year (36 month term) lease for a boring generic car that has a sticker price of $24,600 (MSRP−Manufacturer's Suggested Retail Price).

You have managed to negotiate the price down to $23,000 (Cap. Cost). You decide not to make a down payment but you have a trade-in worth $5,000. Your *Net Cap Cost* is therefore $23,000 *minus* $5,000, which equals $18,000.

Now, the Dealer tells you (because you asked) that the *Money Factor* is *0.00375* (0.00375 x 2400 = 9.0%) and the Residual Percentage is 60% of MSRP. The Residual amount in dollars is 0.60 *multiplied by* $24,600, which equals $14,760.

- Depreciation Fee: ($18,000 *minus* $14,760) *divided by* 36 = $90
- Finance Fee: ($18,000 *plus* $14,760) *multiplied by* 0.00375 = $122.85
- Monthly Lease Payment: $90 *plus* $122.85 = $212.85
- Note the effect of the money factor on the amount of the Monthly Lease Payment. The following example decreases the factor:
- Finance Fee: ($18,000 *plus* $14,760) *multiplied by* 0.00262 = $85.83
- New Monthly Lease Payment: $90 *plus* $85.83 = $175.83
- APR is 6.2% rather than 9% which saves the lessor $212.82 *minus* $175.63 *equals* $37.22 per month and $1,339.92 over the lease term.

Note the interest payment is the average amount paid over the life of the lease. Actually, the interest amount decreases over time. The interest part of a monthly payment is calculated:

$$\text{Interest (i)} = P - (1 - r)i - 1\,(P - Cr)$$

i = month

P = payment

r = monthly interest rate

C = loan amount

Finance Fees: Payment for use of the leasing company's money. This is calculated as follows:

Finance Fee = (Net Cap Cost + Residual) x Money Factor

Monthly Finance Fee, also called Money Factor, is calculated as follows:

Interest Rate = 24 x Money Factor (expressed as APR)

Example 1:

APR = 24 x 0.0020625

APR = 0.495

APR = 4.95%

Example 2:

APR = 24 x 0.00262

APR = 0.062

APR = 6.2%

Chapter Three

The Security Agreement

A. Creation of a Security Interest

Example and Questions

Let's return to the Law Student. After using his extra money to purchase the car, the Student needs a $25,000 loan to attend Law School his last year. The Bank is eager to make the loan if certain conditions are met at a very low interest rate (2.4%). Other than having the loan guaranteed by someone with an income, the Bank wants collateral of which Student has not much.

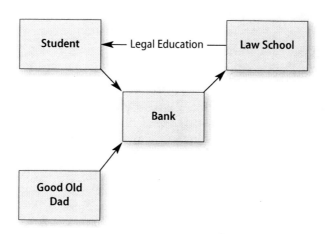

Questions

Problem 3.1

➢ What does the Student give the bank?

Problem 3.2

➤ What does Good Old Dad give the Bank?

Problem 3.3

➤ Apply the definitions of Debtor in §9-102(a)(28) and Obligor in §9-102(a)(59) to both Good Old Dad and Student.

Notice to Co-Signers in Consumer Transactions

The following clause is included in co-signer agreements to ensure that they are neither unfair nor deceptive:

> You are being asked to *guarantee* this debt. Think carefully before you do. If the borrower doesn't pay the debt, you will have to. Be sure you can afford to pay if you have to, and that you want to accept this responsibility.
>
> You may have to pay up to the full amount of the debt if the borrower does not pay. You may also have to pay late fees or collection costs, which increases the amount.
>
> The Creditor can collect this debt from you without first trying to collect from the borrower. The Creditor can use the same collection methods against you that can be used against the borrower, such as suing you, garnishing your wages, etc. *This debt will be a part of your credit record.*

This notice is not the contract that makes you liable for the debt. *See,* 16 C.F.R. 444.3 (Federal Trade Commission Consumer Credit Practices Rules).

A creditor who obligates a surety in connection with the extension of consumer credit in or affecting commerce without giving the surety this notice is guilty of a deceptive act or practice within the meaning of the Federal Trade Commission Act. Banks are generally beyond the Federal Trade Commission's jurisdiction, but the Federal Reserve Board and the Federal Home Loan Bank Board, which between themselves regulate most of the nation's banks and savings institutions, have adopted substantially similar rules requiring the same kind of notice to sureties. 12 C.F.R. 227.14 & 535.3. Some states, by their local law, require the same or a similar warning to consumer sureties. *See,* Uniform Consumer Credit Code (U.C.C.C.) 3.208.

B. Granting a Security Interest by Pledge

Example and Questions

The Student determines that he needs more money for his living expenses, and he goes to the Pawn Shop and pawns (pledges) his mountain bike receiving $300. The Student has a minimum of forty days to redeem the mountain bike, after which the Pawn Shop may sell to a buyer. Note that the Official Code of Georgia (O.C.G.A.) provides a ten-day grace period under §44-14-403(b)(1) and 30 additional days under §44-14-403(b)(2).

Questions

Problem 3.4

➢ At the time of the pawn of the bike, what is the status of the Pawn Shop?

➢ What is a pledge?

➢ How does the Student redeem the bike?

Problem 3.5

➢ Is the Pawn Shop required to have a written security agreement to assert a security interest? If not, why not?

Problem 3.6

➢ What must be in an agreement to make it a security agreement?

Problem 3.7

➢ What is it about a conditional sale agreement, an Article 9 consignment (§9-102(20)), or a security agreement disguised as a lease that causes those transactions to be treated as security agreements?

➢ Where is the grant of an interest in property from a debtor to a secured party?

C. Article 9 Consignments

As to "consignment" within the scope of Article 9, see Comment 6 to §9-109, which states:

> 6. *Consignments.* Subsection (a)(4) is new. This Article applies to every "consignment." The term, defined in Section 9-102, includes many but not all "true" consignments (i.e., bailments for the purpose of sale). If a transaction is a "sale or return," as defined in Section 2-326, it is not a "consignment." In a "sale or return" transaction, the buyer becomes the owner of the goods, and the seller may obtain an enforceable security interest in the goods only by satisfying the requirements of Section 9-203.
>
> Under common law, creditors of a bailee were unable to reach the interest of the bailor (in the case of a consignment, the consignor-owner). Like former Section 2-326 and former Article 9, this Article changes the common law result; however, it does so in a different manner. For purposes of determining the rights and interests of third-party creditors of, and purchasers of the goods from, the consignee, but not for other purposes, such as remedies of the consignor, the consignee is deemed to acquire under this Article whatever rights and title the consignor had or had to transfer. *See,* Section 9-319. The interest of a consignor is defined to be a security interest under revised Section 1-201(b)(35) [In Georgia 1-201(37)], more specifically, a purchase-money security interest in the consignee's inventory. *See,* Section 9-103(d). Thus, the rules pertaining to lien creditors, buyers, and attachment, perfection, and priority of competing security interests apply to consigned goods. The relationship between the consignor and consignee is left to other law. Consignors also have no duties under Part 6. *See,* Section 9-601(g).
>
> Sometimes parties characterize transactions that secure an obligation (other than the bailee's obligation to returned bailed goods) as "consignments." These transactions are not "consignments" as contemplated by Section 9-109(a)(4). See Section 9-102. This Article applies also to these transactions, by virtue of Section 9-109(a)(1). They create a security interest within the meaning of the first sentence of Section 1-201(b)(35) [In Georgia 1-201(37)].
>
> This Article does not apply to bailments for sale that fall outside the definition of "consignment" in Section 9-102 and that do not create a security interest that secures an obligation.

Questions

Problem 3.8

➢ Review the definition of an Article 9 consignment in §9-102(20). Quite clearly a consignment is usually thought of as a transaction whereby the owner of goods delivers those goods to a third party for the purpose of sale to a member of the public. How does a consignment as above understood differ from a *sale or return* under §2-326(b)?

Problem 3.9

➢ How does a consignment as above understood differ from a *sale on approval* as defined in §2-326(a)?

Problem 3.10

➢ Does the Article 9 definition of consignment apply to *consignment shop* located in a number of strip malls?

➢ In other words, does Article 9 apply to the goods generally consigned therein? Explain.

Problem 3.11

➢ If a client wishes to consign some antique cabinets to a Furniture Store, what should an attorney advise that client to do?

Problem 3.12

➢ If the Furniture Store's inventory is subject to a perfected security interest by The Bank covering "all inventory now held or herein after acquired," what should the consignor do?

D. Attachment of a Security Interest

Section 9-203 provides for attachment and enforceability of security interests. The section states:

(a) *Attachment.* A security interest attaches to collateral when it becomes enforceable against the debtor with respect to the collateral, unless an agreement expressly postpones the time of attachment.

(b) *Enforceability.* Except as otherwise provided in subsections (c) through (i), a security interest is enforceable against the debtor and third parties with respect to the collateral only if:

(1) value has been given;

(2) the debtor has rights in the collateral or the power to transfer rights in the collateral to a secured party; and

(3) one of the following conditions is met:

(A) the debtor has authenticated a security agreement that provides a description of the collateral and, if the security interest covers timber to be cut, a description of the land concerned;

(B) the collateral is not a certificated security and is in the possession of the secured party under Section 9-313 pursuant to the debtor's security agreement;

(C) the collateral is a certificated security in registered form and the security certificate has been delivered to the secured party under Section 8-301 pursuant to the debtor's security agreement; or

(D) the collateral is deposit accounts, electronic chattel paper, investment property, or letter-of-credit rights, and the secured party has control under Section 9-104, 9-105, 9-106, or 9-107 pursuant to the debtor's security agreement.

Note that *Value* is defined in §§ 1-204 and 9-102(57). Read the sections carefully to understand the definitions.

The debtor's *Rights in the Collateral* may be less than unencumbered title. Section 9-203(b)(3) contains a list of four conditions that must be met in addition to the requirements for value and the debtor having a transferable interest in the personal property being used as collateral.

Questions

Problem 3.13

➢ What act is required of a secured party under § 9-203(b)(3)(A)? *See also*, § 9-102(a)(7), "Authenticate."

Problem 3.14

➢ What act is required under § 9-203(b)(3)(B)?

Problem 3.15

➢ What act is required under § 9-203(b)(3)(C)?

Problem 3.16

➢ What act is required under § 9-203(b)(3)(D)?

Problem 3.17

➢ Does the Security Agreement always need to be in writing? If not, what may substitute for the writing? *See* § 1-201(3), definition of "Agreement."

Problem 3.18

➤ What if no formal security agreement was ever signed by a debtor?

➤ May a security interest still be enforced by applying the "composite document" rule, that is, by combining various documents to establish the grant of a security interest sufficient to be enforceable against third parties to the transaction? *See* the following opinion.

In re Bollinger Corp.

614 F.2d 924 (3rd Cir. 1980) (edited; most citations omitted;
current code references are in brackets)

ROSENN, Circuit Judge

[In *In re Bollinger Corp.*, the Debtor Bollinger executed a promissory note containing the following:]

> Security. This Promissory Note is secured by security interests in a certain Security Agreement between Bollinger and Industrial Credit Company ... and in a Financing Statement filed by (ICC)..., and is further secured by security interests in a certain security agreement to be delivered by Bollinger to Z and J with this Promissory Note covering the identical machinery and equipment as identified in the ICC Agreement and with identical schedule attached in the principal amount of Eighty-Five Thousand Dollars. ($85,000).

[In a contest pitting the trustee in bankruptcy against Z&J over the proceeds from the sale of the collateral, the appeals court sided with Z&J.]

Question

Problem 3.19

➤ In challenging Z&J's claim to be a secured creditor, what status was being claimed by the trustee? *See*, Bankruptcy Code § 544.

[The Court explained that] [u]nder Article Nine of the U.C.C., two documents are generally required to create a perfected security interest in a debtor's collateral. First, there must be a "security agreement" giving the creditor an interest in the collateral. Section 9-203(1)(b) [9-203(b)(1)] contains minimal requirements for the creation of a security agreement. In order to create a security agreement, there must be: (1) a writing (2) signed by the debtor (3) containing a description of the collateral or the types of collateral. Section 9-203, Comment 1. The requirements of section 9-203(1)(b) [9-203(b)(1)] further two basic policies. First, an evidentiary function is served by requiring a signed security agreement and second, a written agreement also obviates any Statute of Frauds problems with the debtor-creditor relationship. Id. Comments 3, 5. The second document generally required is a "financing statement," which is a document signed by both parties and filed for public record. The financing statement serves the purpose of giving public notice to other creditors that a security interest is claimed in the debtor's collateral.

Despite the minimal formal requirements set forth in section 9-203 for the creation of a security agreement, the commercial world has frequently neglected to comply with this simple Code provision. Soon after Article Nine's enactment, creditors who had failed to obtain formal security agreements, but who nevertheless had obtained and filed financing statements, sought to enforce secured claims. Under section 9-402 [9-502], a security agreement may serve as a financing statement if it is signed by both parties. The question arises whether the converse is true: Can a signed financing statement operate as a security agreement? The earliest case to consider this question was American Card Co. v. H.M.H. Co., 97 R.I. 59, 196 A.2d 150, 152 (1963) which held that a financing statement could not operate as a security agreement because there was no language granting a security interest to a creditor. Although section 9-203(1)(b) [9-203(b)(1)] makes no mention of such a grant language requirement, the court in American Card thought that implicit in the definition of "security agreement" under section 9-105(1)(h) [9-102(73)] was such a requirement; some grant language was necessary to "create or provide security."

* * *

In the case before us, the district court went a step further and held that the promissory note executed by Bollinger in favor of Z&J, standing alone, was sufficient to act as the security agreement between the parties. In so doing, the court implicitly rejected the American Card rule requiring grant language before a security agreement arises under section 9-203(1)(b) [9-203(b)(1)]. The parties have not referred to any Pennsylvania state cases on the question and our independent research has failed to uncover any. But although we agree that no formal grant of a security interest need exist before a security agreement arises, we do not think that the promissory note standing alone would be sufficient under Pennsylvania law to act as the security agreement. We believe, however, that the promissory note, read in conjunction with the financing statement duly filed and supported, as it is here, by correspondence during the course of the transaction between the parties, would be sufficient under Pennsylvania law to establish a valid security agreement.

* * *

Question

Problem 3.20

> ➤ On what basis is the court holding that a security interest was indeed created? *See* the following discussion.

[The Court further stated], [w]hen the parties have neglected to sign a separate security agreement, it would appear that the better and more practical view is to look at the transaction as a whole in order to determine if there is a writing, or writings, signed by the debtor describing the collateral which demonstrates an intent to create a security interest in the collateral. In connection with Z&J's loan of $150,000 to Bollinger, the relevant writings to be considered are: (1) the promissory note; (2) the financing statement; (3) a group of letters constituting the course of dealing between the parties. The district court focused solely on the promissory note finding it sufficient to constitute the security agreement. Reference, however, to the language in the note reveals that the note standing alone cannot serve as the security agreement. The note recites that along with the assigned 1972 security agreement between Bollinger and ICC, the Z&J loan is "further secured by security interests in a certain Security Agreement to be delivered by Bollinger to Z&J with this Promissory Note, …" (Emphasis added.) The bankruptcy judge correctly reasoned that "(t)he intention to create a separate security agreement negates any inference that the debtor intended that the promissory note constitute the security agreement. At best, the note is some evidence that a security agreement was contemplated by the parties, but by its own terms, plainly indicates that it is not the security agreement."

Looking beyond the promissory note, Z&J did file a financing statement signed by Bollinger containing a detailed list of all the collateral intended to secure the $150,000 loan to Bollinger. The financing statement alone meets the basic section 9-203 requirements of a writing, signed by the debtor, describing the collateral. However, the financing statement provides only an inferential basis for concluding that the parties intended a security agreement. There would be little reason to file such a detailed financing statement unless the parties intended to create a security interest. The intention of the parties to create a security interest may be gleaned from the expression of future intent to create one in the promissory note and the intention of the parties as expressed in letters constituting their course of dealing.

The promissory note was executed by Bollinger in favor of Z&J in December 1974. Prior to the consummation of the loan, Z&J sent a letter to Bollinger on May 30, 1974, indicating that the loan would be made "provided" Bollinger secured the loan by a mortgage on its machinery and equipment. Bollinger sent a letter to Z&J on September 19, 1974, indicating:

> With your (Z&J's) stated desire to obtain security for material and funds advanced, it would appear that the use of the note would answer both our problems. Since the draft forwarded to you offers full collateralization for the funds to be advanced under it and bears normal interest during its term, it should offer you maximum security.

Subsequent to the execution of the promissory note, Bollinger sent to Z&J a list of the equipment and machinery intended as collateral under the security agreement which was to be, but never was, delivered to Z&J. In November 1975, the parties exchanged letters clarifying whether Bollinger could substitute or replace equipment in the ordinary course of business without Z&J's consent. Such a clarification would not have been necessary had a security interest not been intended by the parties. Finally, a letter of November 18, 1975, from Bollinger to Z&J indicated that "any attempted impairment of the collateral would constitute an event of default."

From the course of dealing between Z&J and Bollinger, we conclude there is sufficient evidence that the parties intended a security agreement to be created separate from the assigned ICC agreement with Bollinger. All the evidence points towards the intended creation of such an agreement and since the financing statement contains a detailed list of the collateral, signed by Bollinger, we hold that a valid Article Nine security agreement existed....

* * *

Questions

Problem 3.21

➤ Who does the trustee in bankruptcy represent?

Problem 3.22

➤ If you were the attorney for the trustee, what would you argue to avoid the security interest?

In re Flager

2007 WL 1701812 (Bankr. M.D. Ga. 2007)
(edited; most citations omitted)

WALKER, United States Bankruptcy Judge

This matter comes before the Court on Terry and Larry Hortman's objection to confirmation. This is a core matter within the meaning of 28 U.S.C.

§ 157(b)(2)(L). After considering the pleadings, the evidence, and the applicable authorities, the Court enters the following findings of fact and conclusions of law in conformance with Federal Rule of Bankruptcy Procedure 7052.

FINDINGS OF FACT

Debtor, Vernon Max Flager, Jr., filed a Chapter 13 petition on February 7, 2007. On Schedule D, he listed Terry Hortman as a secured creditor with a lien on a 1993 GMC Sierra pickup truck. Larry Hortman filed a proof of claim (claim no. 1) in the name of "Terry or Larry Hortman," showing a secured claim of $9,750, secured by a vehicle valued at $4,700. (Creditor's ex. 2.)

Debtor's proposed plan made no provision to pay Larry Hortman as a secured creditor. The Hortmans, who are brothers, objected to confirmation of the plan because it proposed to pay their claim as unsecured with a 0% dividend. Debtor opposed the objection on the ground that Debtor never gave the Hortmans a security interest in the GMC truck.

The debt arose because Larry Hortman advanced Debtor the money to purchase the GMC truck. On May 27 and 28, 2002, Debtor and the Hortmans executed a number of documents memorializing the debt. First, Debtor signed a handwritten document titled "Promissory Note" and dated May 28, 2007, that provided as follows:

> For value received, [sic] the undersigned promises to pay to the holder of this note Larry G. Hortman the sum of $9750.00 nine thousand seven hundred & fifty dollars. This amount includes 600.00 six hundred dollars interest.

> This note shall be paid in 9 nine consecutive payments of one thousand dollars $1000.00 with the first payment due on July 1, 2002. The final payment of $750.00 seven hundred & fifty dollars paid at the end of the note.

> The undersigned maker may repay this note in whole or in part without penalty.

> This contract shall be constituted [sic] in all respects and enforced according to the laws of the state of Georgia.

Second, Debtor executed a "Buyers Order" dated May 27, 2002, from Autos Unlimited for the purchase of the GMC truck for a total cost of $6,000, including vehicle price, tax, and title fee. (Creditors' ex. 2.) Third, Debtor signed a "Due Bill" for certain work to be performed on the GMC truck as a condition of the purchase. (Creditors' ex. 2.) Fourth, Debtor signed a "Title Application" for the GMC truck, dated May 27, 2002, that listed Larry G. Hortman as a lienholder. (Creditors' ex. 2.) Fifth, Debtor signed a "Limited Power of

Attorney For Completing Motor Vehicle Transactions," dated May 27, 2002, for purposes of obtaining a certificate of title. (Creditors' ex. 2.)

At a hearing held on May 21, 2007, Debtor stipulated to the authenticity of all the documents. In addition, he testified that he signed all the documents on the same day. Debtor testified the note covered the debt for the truck and other debt he owed the Hortmans. He also testified he understood Larry Hortman would have a lien on the truck. Debtor stated he understood when someone has a lien, it means that person has a security interest.

After considering the evidence and the arguments of the parties, the Court will sustain the objection to confirmation.

CONCLUSIONS OF LAW

Pursuant to Article 9 of Georgia's Commercial Code, a creditor may only enforce a security interest in collateral against the debtor and third parties if three requirements are satisfied: (1) the debtor received value; (2) the debtor has rights in the collateral; and (3) "[t]he debtor has authenticated a security agreement that provides a description of the collateral [.]" O.C.G.A. § 11-9-203(b)(3)(A). The only requirement in dispute in this case is whether Debtor authenticated a security agreement.

A security agreement is "an agreement that creates or provides for a security interest." *Id.* § 11-9-102(72). Authentication requires the debtor "[t]o sign" or "[t]o execute ... with the present intent of the authenticating person to identify the person and adopt or accept a record." *Id.* § 11-9-102(7). Thus, the need for authentication imposes "an evidentiary requirement in the nature of a Statute of Frauds." U.C.C. § 9-203, cmt. 3.

In *In re Hollie*, 42 B.R. 111 (Bankr.M.D.Ga.1984), the court said, "Georgia law ... does not require 'magic words' to create a valid security interest. A clause that specifically grants a party a security interest is not necessary. Rather, the Court must refer to the general law of contracts and determine whether the parties intended to create a security agreement." *Id.* at 117 (citing *Barton v. Chemical Bank*, 577 F.2d 1329 (11th Cir.1978)). *See also, In re Seibold*, 351 B.R. 741, 745–46 (Bankr. D. Idaho 2006); *In re Sabol*, 337 B.R. 195, 198 (Bankr.C.D.Ill.2006). The court in *Trust Company Bank v. Walker (In re Walker)*, 35 B.R. 237 (Bankr.N.D.Ga.1983), reached a similar conclusion about Georgia law, stating, "A security agreement need not be in any particular form" so long as it consists of a writing signed by the debtor that reasonably describes the collateral and includes language evidencing an intent to create a security interest. *Id.* at 239–240. Furthermore, the security agreement need not be enshrined in one document. For example, "a financing statement alone cannot serve as a 'security agreement.' ... [H]owever, [courts] recognize that a financing statement attended by other documents or circumstances may suffice as a valid 'security agreement.'" *In re Carmichael Enter., Inc.,* 334 F.Supp. 94, 104–05 (N.D.Ga.1971) (internal citations omitted).

In *Hollie,* the court found the contract at issue was a security agreement that created a security interest. 42 B.R. at 117. The contract did not include a specific clause granting a security interest. However, it was titled a "security agreement," it referred to the creditor as the secured party, and it provided its purpose and intent were to secure a note. *Id.*

The facts of this case are not quite as persuasive. Nevertheless, they lead the Court to the same conclusion reached in *Hollie.* Debtor signed a note acknowledging a debt to Larry Hortman, signed a bill of sale for the purchase of a truck, and— most significantly—signed a title application with a detailed description of the collateral that listed Larry Hortman as a lienholder. Taken together, these three documents demonstrate the parties' intent to create a security interest. This conclusion is supported by Debtor's testimony that he understood he was giving Larry Hortman a lien on the truck until the note—which included amounts loans for purchase of the truck—was satisfied and that the lien evidenced a security interest.

Debtor has argued the documents are ineffective to create a security interest because they are unclear about which debt is covered by the lien. Debtor owes multiple debts to the Hortmans, including an unsecured debt for rent, as demonstrated by a separate proof of claim they filed in this case. However, the evidence indicates Debtor signed the promissory note in conjunction with purchasing the truck and giving Larry Hortman a lien on the truck. Although the title application and note were dated one day apart, Debtor testified he signed them on the same day and understood the lien would continue until he paid off the note. Consequently, the Court is persuaded that Debtor intended the lien to secure the note.

For the foregoing reasons, the Court finds the parties entered into a security agreement. Because there is no dispute that the other requirements for an enforceable security interest are satisfied, the Hortmans are entitled to treatment as secured creditors for purposes of claim no. 1, and the Court will sustain their objection to confirmation.

* * *

Question

Problem 3.23

➢ In enforcing the security interest of the Hortmans, what did the court find was determinative?

E. Description of the Collateral

Section 9-108(a)'s black letter rule provides that a description is sufficient "if it reasonably identifies what is described." Examples of "reasonable identification" are listed in §9-108(b). Note particularly §9-108(c) and (e). Compare the sufficiency of description for the grant of a security interest with the sufficiency of the description for the purposes of the financing statement under §9-504.

Questions

Problem 3.24

➤ Although a serial number for a piece of equipment used on collateral is not required, why might it be a good idea?

Problem 3.25

➤ When is an after-acquired property clause not necessary to describe covered collateral? *See,* §9-204.

In re Pickle Logging, Inc.

286 B.R. 181 (Bankr. M.D. Ga. 2002)
(edited; most citations omitted)

LANEY, United States Bankruptcy Judge

Pickle Logging, Inc. ("Debtor") is an Americus, Georgia based company doing business in the tree logging industry. In an effort to cure an arrearage to Deere Credit, Inc. ("Movant"), Debtor refinanced eight pieces of equipment. The refinancing was done with Movant.

On April 18, 2002, Debtor filed for Chapter 11 bankruptcy protection. Prior to the bankruptcy filing, in addition to the refinancing mentioned above, Debtor had put the same eight pieces of equipment, as well as other assets, up as collateral in transactions with other creditors. Because there were multiple security interests in the eight pieces of equipment, Debtor filed motions to determine the secured status of a number of different creditors. After consent orders resolved much of the conflict between secured creditors as to priority and extent of security interests, the final issue remained as to the value of the eight pieces of equipment. The values assigned to each piece of equipment would determine the amount due to the secured creditors for adequate protection.

At a hearing held on August 16, 2002 and the continued hearing on August 21, 2002 to determine the value of the eight pieces of equipment, the present issue was raised: whether Movant had a perfected security interest in one specific piece of equipment, a 548G skidder serial number DW548GX568154 ("548

G skidder"), which had been mislabeled in both the financing statement and the security agreement as a 648G skidder, serial number DW648GX568154. After hearing testimony from expert witnesses that a 548G skidder is substantially different in appearance, performance, and price from a 648G skidder, the court held that Movant did not have a perfected security interest in the 548G skidder because of the mislabeling.

Movant contends that the mislabeling is not seriously misleading because it is off by only one digit. Movant urges that a person of ordinary business prudence would be put on notice to inquire further about the 548G skidder despite the mislabeling. Therefore, Movant has a perfected security interest in the 548G skidder and would not be subordinate to [the Debtor in possession exercising the rights and powers of a trustee].

Debtor argues first that the 548G skidder owned by Debtor is not listed in the security agreement or the financing statement, therefore Movant does not have a security interest in the 548G skidder. Furthermore, Debtor argues that a person of ordinary business prudence would know that a 548G skidder differs substantially from a 648G skidder. Debtor contends that the mislabeling is seriously misleading because of the difference in the two models. Debtor argues that there is nothing patently erroneous about the serial number listed on the security agreement or the financing statement to put a person of ordinary business prudence on notice to inquire further. Finally, Debtor contends that, in order for a secured party to have a security interest in a piece of collateral, the security agreement must include a valid description of the collateral. Under contract law, Movant might have the right to reform the contract. However, because of the Chapter 11 bankruptcy proceeding, this remedy is not available to Movant. Even with reformation, Debtor, with the status of a lien creditor, would have higher priority than Movant would receive with a reformed security agreement.

CONCLUSIONS OF LAW

Under the Bankruptcy Code ("Code"), a debtor-in-possession has the same rights and powers as a trustee. *See* 11 U.S.C. §1107. Additionally, under the "strong arm" provision of 11 U.S.C. §544(a)(1), a debtor-in-possession acquires the status of a hypothetical lien creditor, deemed to be perfected as of the filing date of the bankruptcy petition. 11 U.S.C. §544(a)(1); *see also First American Bank & Trust Company of Athens, Georgia v. Harris (In re Stewart)*, 74 B.R. 350, 353–354 (Bankr.M.D.Ga.1987).

Under Georgia law, the definition of a lien creditor includes a trustee in bankruptcy. *See* O.C.G.A. §11-9-102(a)(53)(C). Since a debtor-in-possession acquires the same rights and powers as a trustee, a debtor-in-possession has the status of a lien creditor under Georgia law as well. *See generally, WWG Industries, Inc. v. United Textiles, Inc. (In re WWG Industries, Inc.)*, 772 F.2d 810, 811–812 (11th Cir.1985). Further, under Georgia law, a party with an unperfected security interest is subordinate to a lien creditor. *See* O.C.G.A. § 11-9-317(a)(2)(B). The question is whether Movant's security interest in the 548G skidder is perfected despite the mislabeling on the security agreement and the financing statement.

Pursuant to O.C.G.A. § 11-9-203(b)(3)(A), a security interest in collateral is not enforceable against the debtor or third parties unless the debtor has signed, executed, or otherwise adopted a security agreement that contains a description of the collateral. O.C.G.A. § 11-9-203(b)(3)(A); *see also* O.C.G.A. § 11-9-102(a)(7). The description of the collateral in the security agreement and the financing statement, if required, must comport with O.C.G.A. § 11-9-108(a). O.C.G.A. § 11-9-108(a); *see also* O.C.G.A. § 11-9-504(1). The description of collateral is sufficient if it reasonably identifies what is described. *See* O.C.G.A. § 11-9-108(a). "The question of the sufficiency of [a] description of [collateral] in a [recorded document] is one of law...." *Bank of Cumming v. Chapman*, 245 Ga. 261, 264 S.E.2d 201 (1980), quoting *First National Bank of Fitzgerald v. Spicer*, 10 Ga.App. 503(1), 73 S.E. 753 (1912).

Any number of things could be used to describe collateral and satisfy O.C.G.A. § 11-9-108(a). A physical description of the collateral, including or excluding a serial number, could be used so long as it "reasonably identifies what is described." O.C.G.A. § 11-9-108(a). The description merely needs to raise a red flag to a third party indicating that more investigation may be necessary to determine whether or not an item is subject to a security agreement. *See Abney v. I.T.T. Diversified Credit Corporation (In re Environmental Electronic Systems, Inc.)*, 11 B.R. 965, 967 (Bankr.N.D.Ga.1981). A party does not lose its secured status just because the description includes an inaccurate serial number. *See Yancey Brothers Company v. Dehco, Inc.*, 108 Ga.App. 875, 877, 134 S.E.2d 828, 830 (1964). However, if the serial number is inaccurate, there must be additional information that provides a "key" to the collateral's identity. *Id.*

* * *

According to testimony at the August 16, 2002 hearing, Debtor owned more than one of Movant's skidders, including at least two 548G skidders and at least two 648G skidders. There is nothing in either the financing statement or the security agreement that raises a red flag to a third party. A potential purchaser of the 548G skidder in dispute here could easily assume that the skidder is not covered by either the security agreement or the financing statement.

If just the model number was incorrect or if just the serial number was incorrect, the result may be different. It is apparent from the other items listed on the security agreement and the financing statement that the model number is reflected in the serial number. If the model number was not repeated in the serial number, then it would be apparent that something was wrong with one of the two numbers. At a minimum it should raise a red flag to a person of ordinary business prudence that further investigation is necessary. However, with both of the numbers reflecting a 648G skidder, there is nothing to indicate that there was a mistake.

Therefore, the court's order dated September 3, 2002 will not be changed. The 548G skidder is mis-described in both the security agreement and the financing statement. The rights of Debtor, as a hypothetical lien creditor, are superior to the rights of Movant.

Questions

Problem 3.26

➣ Is the security agreement between the Debtor and the Movant effective? Note the Court's reference to reformation.

Problem 3.27

➣ Exactly why does the Debtor prevail?

Problem 3.28

➣ If there had not been a bankruptcy filing and no creditor had a judgment lien against Pickle Logging, might Deere Credit have prevailed? Explain.

Problem 3.29

➣ What if the description in the financing statement (the UCC #1) was accurate?

Problem 3.30

➣ What is the difference with regard to function between a financing statement and a security agreement?

Note the limitations in § 9-108(e), "when description by type insufficient." Read Comment 5 to § 9-108.

In re Jojo's 10 Restaurant, LLC

455 B.R. 321 (Bankr. D. Mass. 2011) (edited; citations omitted, additional text included in brackets)
HOFFMAN, Bankruptcy Judge

PROCEDURAL BACKGROUND

On April 4, 2010, the debtor commenced this case by filing a petition for relief under Chapter 11 of the Bankruptcy Code, 11 U.S.C. §§ 101–1532. On May 25, 2010, the debtor commenced this adversary proceeding against Devin and four other secured creditors seeking (i) a declaratory judgment avoiding each defendant's security interest in the assets of the debtor for lack of perfection and determining the amount owed to each defendant (Count I), (ii) a judgment avoiding each defendant's security interest pursuant to Bankruptcy Code § 544 (Count II) and (iii) an order preserving for the bankruptcy estate any interest in the avoided liens pursuant to Bankruptcy Code § 551 (Count III). Devin filed an answer and counterclaim seeking a declaratory judgment as to the validity, security and amount of the debtor's obligation to it. On January 12, 2011, the main case was converted to one under Chapter 7 of the Bankruptcy Code [and a trustee was appointed replacing the debtor-in-possession].

* * *

FACTUAL BACKGROUND

The relevant facts are not in dispute. On May 15, 2009, the debtor and Devin entered into, among other agreements, a commercial lease agreement, an asset purchase agreement, a bill of sale, a promissory note and a pledge agreement by which the debtor leased space and purchased assets in order to operate a restaurant in Devin's building in Maynard, Massachusetts. The equipment sold by Devin to the debtor had been acquired by Devin in connection with a prior restaurant operating at the premises. Devin financed the asset purchase transaction.

Pursuant to the asset purchase agreement, the debtor agreed to pay $285,000 to purchase all of Devin's assets used in the former restaurant including inventory, furniture, fixtures and equipment (the "Physical Assets"). The agreement also provided for the transfer to the debtor of all transferrable licenses issued in Devin's name, including the former restaurant's liquor license issued by the town of Maynard.

* * *

In payment of a portion of the purchase price, the debtor gave Devin a non-interest bearing promissory note dated May 15, 2009 in the amount of $225,000, payable within sixty months of execution. The promissory note refers to "collateral given to the Lender to secure this Note," thereby indicating that the parties understood that the loan was to be collateralized. The note does not, however, identify specific collateral or contain any language affirmatively granting to Devin a security interest.

The parties signed a pledge agreement whereby the debtor agreed to pledge its liquor license to Devin as security for its obligations under the promissory note. The parties agree that neither party received approval of the pledge in accordance with Mass. Gen. Laws ch. 138, § 23.

Section 5 of the asset purchase agreement, entitled "Security Documents," referring to the promissory note, commercial lease and liquor license, provides that "said Note and Commercial Lease Agreement shall be secured by a standard form U.C.C. Security Agreement and perfected by a standard form U.C.C. Financing Statement [and] a pledge against the Full Beverage Liquor License approved by the Town of Maynard...." [Which was properly recorded.] No agreement purporting to be a "U.C.C. Security Agreement" or any similarly-titled document was introduced into the record of this case nor has there been any allegation that such an agreement was entered into.

* * *

POSITION OF THE PARTIES

Devin argues that the agreements summarized above, when taken as a whole, served to create a security interest in its favor in those assets listed in the rider to the financing statement, which security interest was duly perfected upon the recording of the financing statement with the secretary of the commonwealth. The trustee argues that the debtor failed to grant Devin a security interest in any of its assets[1] other than the liquor license and that with respect to the liquor license Devin failed to properly perfect its security interest. The trustee asserts his status as a hypothetical lien creditor under Bankruptcy Code § 544 to seek to avoid Devin's security interest.

---

1. In the complaint, which was filed before the case was converted from Chapter 11 to one under Chapter 7, the debtor alleged that Devin's security interest is unperfected and is therefore voidable by the debtor, in its capacity as a debtor in possession. In his motion for partial summary judgment the trustee appears to have adopted a different theory of the case arguing that Devin's security interest in the Physical Assets is invalid, not merely unperfected.

Bankruptcy Code § 544 endows a trustee with so-called "strong-arm" powers that enable the trustee to avoid certain prepetition liens against property of the debtor. Section 544(a) confers on a trustee the right to seek to avoid any transfer of property or obligation incurred by a debtor that is voidable by the holder of a judicial lien or execution against the debtor or a bona fide purchaser for value of real estate as of the date of case commencement.

The U.C.C. governs the creation of security interests. To be effective, a security interest must have attached to the collateral in question. U.C.C. § 9-308(a). Unless an agreement between the parties provides otherwise, a security interest attaches to collateral only when it becomes enforceable against a debtor with respect to the collateral. § 9-203(a). A security interest in a debtor's assets becomes enforceable when (i) value has been given, (ii) the debtor has rights in the collateral or the power to transfer the rights and (iii) the debtor has authenticated a security agreement that provides a description of the collateral. § 9-203(b). In order for a security interest to have priority over subsequent secured creditors, it must be perfected. § 9-317(a). An attached security interest is perfected upon the filing of a financing statement in the appropriate centralized registry. §§ 9-308(a) and 9-310(a).

With respect to the liquor license, Mass. Gen. Laws ch. 138, § 23 permits a licensee to pledge its interest in the license as collateral for a loan "provided approval of such loan and pledge is given by the local licensing authority and the [Massachusetts Alcoholic Beverage Control Commission (the 'ABCC')]."

* * *

DISCUSSION

Whether the trustee may avoid Devin's security interest in the debtor's property requires a determination as to whether the security interest is enforceable with respect to the collateral under the three-part test of U.C.C. § 9-203(b). There is no dispute that by loaning money to the debtor, Devin gave value to the debtor in exchange for a security interest in both the Physical Assets and the liquor license, thereby satisfying the first test for enforceability. Applying the remaining tests under § 9-203(b) requires examining the Physical Assets and liquor license separately.

With respect to the Physical Assets, there is no dispute that having acquired those assets by way of the bill of sale, the debtor had sufficient "rights in the collateral" to satisfy the second requirement for enforceability under § 9-203(b). Rights in the collateral refers to the debtor's gaining possession of the collateral pursuant to agreement giving him any interest other than naked possession. It is the third requirement, for an authenticated security agreement, that underpins the trustee's position that Devin's security interest in the Physical Assets is unenforceable.

The drafters of the U.C.C. included the requirement to authenticate a security agreement to prevent disputes from arising over which assets are intended to serve as collateral. Massachusetts law does not require that an agreement be entitled security agreement as long as it contains a description of the collateral and it evidences an intent to create a security interest in that collateral. In fact, the security agreement may consist of several different documents that "collectively establish an intention to grant a security interest" in the collateral identified in the documents. If one such document lists the collateral to be secured, it must contain some granting language expressing the debtor's intent to create a security interest.

None of the transaction documents in the present case (except the pledge agreement, which applies only to the liquor license) contains language in which the debtor grants a security interest to Devin. The asset purchase agreement and the related bill of sale identify the assets purchased by the debtor, but neither contains a grant of a security interest or indicates which, if any, of those assets are intended to become collateral for Devin's loan. In fact, the asset purchase agreement states that the relevant grant will be by means of a separate security agreement. No such agreement has been produced. The only document in the record that identifies collateral is the financing statement, but it was signed by Devin only and cannot possibly be construed to reflect the debtor's intent to grant a security interest in such collateral. Without an authenticated security agreement, the secured transaction between the debtor and Devin fails the third test for enforceability under §9-203(b). Accordingly Devin's security interest in the Physical Assets never attached as required by §9-203(a).

With respect to the pledge of the liquor license, the debtor authenticated the pledge agreement by signing it, thus satisfying the third requirement for enforceability under §9-203(b). It does not appear, however, that the debtor had sufficient rights in the liquor license to satisfy the second test of the statute. Mass. Gen. Laws ch. 138, §23 requires that a debtor must receive approval from both the local licensing authority and the state ABCC before a liquor license may be pledged.

These and other cases on this subject rely on a 1976 amendment to Mass. Gen. Laws ch. 138, §23. Prior to that amendment, it was accepted that the holder of a liquor license had no property rights in the license. So for example, the state could revoke an outstanding liquor license without violating the licensee's due process rights. The 1976 amendment created a limited property right in favor of a liquor licensee by permitting the licensee to pledge the license as collateral for a loan, but only with the approval of the licensing authorities. Thus a debtor never acquires independent rights in a Massachusetts liquor license for purposes of satisfying U.C.C. §9-201(b)(ii) unless and until there is a pledge and that pledge has been approved by the required authorities under Mass. Gen. Laws ch. 138, §23. As the debtor in this case failed to secure the necessary governmental approvals to pledge the liquor license to Devin, it did not acquire "rights in the collateral" within the meaning of §9-203(b)(ii). Devin's security interest in the liquor license was, therefore, never enforceable against the debtor, and thus did not attach to the collateral.

* * *

Questions

Problem 3.31

➤ Under Chapter 11, a filing debtor becomes a debtor in possession who exercises rights of a trustee. In that capacity, who is the debtor representing?

Problem 3.32

➤ Devin and the other secured creditors failed to do what to perfect their security interest in the "physical assets?"

Problem 3.33

➤ In §1-201(37), a "security interest" is defined as "an interest in personal property or fixtures which secures payment or performance of an obligation." Section 9-203(b)(3)(A) provides that other than control of or possession of collateral, for attachment to occur "the debtor [will have] authenticated a security agreement...." Section 9-102(73) provides that a "Security Agreement" means an agreement that creates or provides for a security interest. Yet §9-109 as well as §1-201(37) which distinguishes a true lease from a security interest disguised as a lease includes transactions such as "a sale of accounts, chattel paper, payment intangibles [and] promissory notes" and consignments as defined in §9-102(a)(20) within the scope of Article 9. Explain this.

Problem 3.34

➤ Under Massachusetts law is a liquor license property? If so, why was the secured party unperfected?

Georgia has the following statute:

O.C.G.A. §3-3-1. Dealing in alcoholic beverages declared a privilege.

The businesses of manufacturing, distributing, selling, handling, and otherwise dealing in or possessing alcoholic beverages are declared to be privileges in this state and not rights; however, such privileges shall not be exercised except in accordance with the licensing, regulatory, and revenue requirements of this title.

Problem 3.35

➢ What are the three attributes of private personal property?

➢ What attributes of personal property are lacking under the above statute? Note that §§ 9-203(f), (g), (h), and (i) provide for automatic attachment of a security interest once a security interest attaches to the collateral giving rise to the listed collateral.

Problem 3.36

➢ Section 9-203(a) gives a secured party a security interest in proceeds. What are proceeds?

Problem 3.37

➢ Under what circumstances does a security interest not continue in collateral after disposition by a debtor?

➢ Section 9-320 provides that a BIOC "takes free of a security interest created by the buyer's seller, even if the security interest is perfected and the buyer knows of its existence." What characterizes a BIOC?

Problem 3.38

➢ What policy lies behind allowing a BIOC to take free of a security interest created by his seller?

Problem 3.39

➢ Why the exception for a "person buying farm products from a person engaged in farming operations?"

Problem 3.40

➢ What is the exception in § 9-320(b) about?

➢ How do you classify the seller and buyer referred to in that section?

Chapter Four

Perfection and Priority of a Security Interest

A. Perfection

The famous case of *Benedict v. Ratner*, 268 U.S. 353 (1925) established the principal that a security interest wherein the Debtor maintains control of the collateral, not recorded, or otherwise ascertainable by potential creditors was fraudulent. The United States Supreme Court stated "in the case at bar the arrangement for the unfettered use by the company of the proceeds of the accounts precluded the effective creation of a lien and rendered the original assignment fraudulent in law." Note that the United States Supreme Court was referring to a security interest as a lien.

Questions

Problem 4.1

➢ What is the definition of a "lien" for Article 9 purposes? How does such a lien arise? *See* §9-102(52) (definition of "Lien Creditor").

Problem 4.2

➢ How does a lien as defined in Article 9 differ from that of a security interest? *See*, Bankruptcy Code §544 wherein the trustee in bankruptcy can avoid an unperfected security interest for the benefit of the bankruptcy estate.

The Security Agreement constitutes a contract between the Debtor and a Secured Party and is enforceable as between those two parties and unsecured creditors, once the Security Interest attaches. *See*, §9-201(a).

The purpose of perfection is to give notice to third parties, that is, other potential creditors, the trustee in bankruptcy, and lien creditors that there is a secured party who has encumbered certain personal property of the Debtor. *See*, §§ 9-308 to 9-316.

Problem 4.3

➣ Look again at § 9-108, sufficiency of description of collateral for a security agreement, and § 9-504, sufficiency of description for a financing statement. Describe the differences.

➣ What is a super generic description?

Perfection may occur in a number of ways as previously discussed. Filing, possession, control and even automatic perfection are all possibilities depending upon the collateral and the circumstances.

B. Priority

A purchase money security interest ("PMSI") may be taken in consumer goods, equipment, or inventory. Although the rules establishing priority for each differ, the crucial element in establishing the existence of a PMSI is that the value supplied by the creditor enables the debtor to get rights in the collateral involved. *See*, § 9-324. If both the requirements for attachment and perfection are established, a PMSI primes a previously perfected interest covering the same described types of collateral.

Southtrust Bank v. Borg-Warner Acceptance Corp.
760 F.2d 1240 (11th Cir. 1985) (edited; citations omitted, additional text included in brackets)
TUTTLE, Senior Circuit Judge

* * *

[This involves a contest between two-secured parties, Southtrust Bank ("Bank") and Borg-Warner Acceptance Corp. ("BWAC") both of which have perfected security interests in the same collateral (the inventory of a group of now non-existent debtors)]. In each case, the Bank filed its financing statement first. BWAC contends that as a purchase money lender it falls within the purchase money security interest exception to the first to file rule and therefore is entitled to possession of the inventory. BWAC engages in purchase money financing. Here, BWAC purchased invoices from vendors who supplied inventory items to the debtors in question. The security agreements between BWAC and each of the debtors contained the following provision:

> In order to secure repayment to Secured Party of all such extensions of credit made by Secured Party in accordance with this Agreement, and to secure payment of all other debts or liabilities and perform-ance of all obligations of Debtor to Secured Party, whether now ex-isting or hereafter arising, Debtor agrees that Secured Party shall have and hereby grants to Secured Party a security interest in all Inventory of Debtor, whether now owned or hereafter acquired, and all Pro-ceeds and products thereof.

The term "Inventory" was defined as "all inventory, of whatever kind or na-ture, wherever located, now owned or hereafter acquired ... when such in-ventory has been financed by Borg-Warner Acceptance Corporation."

BWAC and the debtors employed a scheduled liquidation arrangement to reduce the debt owed BWAC. Under this arrangement a debtor was permitted to pay a percentage of the invoice each month, without regard to whether the item was actually sold. If an unpaid item was sold, then the remaining inven-tory served as collateral to secure the unpaid balance.

The key issue for decision by this Court is whether inclusion of an after-ac-quired property clause and a future advances clause in BWAC's security agree-ments converted its purchase money security interest (PMSI) into an ordinary security interest.

The district court held that inclusion of after-acquired property and future advances clauses ("the clauses") in the security agreement converted BWAC's PMSI into an ordinary security interest.

* * *

BWAC argues that the cases relied on by the court are distinguishable. First, BWAC notes that almost all the cases following the "transformation" rule (*i.e.,* inclusion of the clauses transforms a PMSI into an ordinary security interest) are consumer bankruptcy cases. It argues that the rationale of those cases, which is to protect the consumer, does not apply in commercial cases such as the case at bar. BWAC argues that the policy considerations in a commercial setting, promoting commercial certainty and encouraging credit extension, do not support the application of the transformation rule. According to BWAC, applying the transformation rule to inventory financiers would require them to police inventory constantly and to see that inventory corresponds on an item-by-item basis with debt.

The Bank argues that the transformation rule is not a product of special bankruptcy considerations, and that if the drafters had intended to limit the rule to consumer transactions, they would have said so, as they did in other sections of the Code. The Bank contends that a holding that inclusion of the clauses destroys a PMSI would not have a serious negative effect on inventory financiers. It points out that such financiers could retain priority by obtaining a subordination agreement from the first-to-file creditor.

We see no reason to limit the holding of *In re Manuel*, [507 F.2d 990 (5th Cir. 1975)] to consumer bankruptcy cases. In that case, the Fifth Circuit stated:

> A plain reading of the statutory requirements would indicate that they require the purchase money security interest to be in the item purchased, and that, as the judges below noted, the purchase money security interest cannot exceed the price of what is purchased in the transaction wherein the security interest is created....

Id. at 993. Nothing in the language of U.C.C. §9-312(3) or §9-107 distinguishes between consumer and commercial transactions or between bankruptcy and non-bankruptcy contexts. We see no policy reasons for creating a distinction where the drafters have not done so.

Second, BWAC contends that the cases supporting the transformation rule involve situations in which the clauses were actually exercised, *e.g., Manuel* (agreement covered pre-existing debt); *Simpson* (future advances actually made). BWAC argues that mere inclusion of the clauses does not void a PMSI. *In re Griffin*, 9 B.R. 880 (Bankr.N.D.Ga.1981) (when creditor is seller, mere existence of unexercised future advances clause does not destroy PMSI). We need not reach the issue of whether mere inclusion of unexercised future advances and after-acquired property clauses voids a PMSI because we find that BWAC exercised the clauses here. After entering the security agreements with the debtors, BWAC regularly purchased inventory for the debtors and now claims that the debtors' BWAC-financed inventory secures these purchases. This is an exercise of the future advances clause. Similarly, BWAC claims as collateral not only the inventory purchased at the time the security agreements were entered, but all BWAC-financed inventory. This is an exercise of the after-acquired property clause. We hold, therefore, that BWAC's exercise of the future advances and after-acquired property clauses in its security agreements with the debtors destroyed its PMSI.

We note, as did the district court, that BWAC retains a security interest in the goods. It merely loses its priority status as a purchase money secured lender. The concept of the floating lien under the U.C.C. remains intact. We hold, merely, that such a floating lien is inconsistent with a PMSI. A PMSI requires a one-to-one relationship between the debt and the collateral.

* * *

Questions

Problem 4.4

➤ In establishing a PMSI priority in inventory, what must the secured creditor do?

Problem 4.5

➤ If the PMSI is claimed in equipment, what must a secured creditor do to establish its priority over a previously perfected secured party who has a security interest in all equipment now owned or after acquired?

Problem 4.6

➤ If the PMSI is in consumer goods, what must the secured party do to establish its priority? *See*, §9-309(1). *But* see, §§9-311(a)(2), (3) and 9-320(b).

Discussion

National Pawn Brokers Unlimited v. Osterman, Inc., 500 N.W.2d 407 (Wis. Ct. App. 1993) dealt with a conditional sales contract between Osterman (jeweler) and Pippin (buyer). Pippin pledged jewelry to National Pawn (a 3rd party) for value, and National Pawn took a security agreement as a good faith purchaser. If the creditor takes a security interest by possession and without a writing, he will lose the security interest if he loses the possession.

Example and Questions

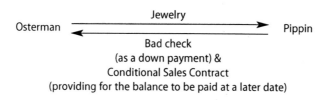

Based on the above transaction, what questions might you as an attorney have? Listed below are some appropriate questions.

Questions

Problem 4.7

➤ What is the status of Osterman?

➤ Is he a merchant, that is, is he in the business of selling jewelry?

➤ Is he selling a piece of jewelry, which he or his family used personally, making the jewelry a consumer good before its sale?

Problem 4.8

➤ What is the status of Pippin?

➤ Is he a consumer buyer? If he is, how might that help Osterman in a contest with the Pawn Shop?

➤ Is he a middleman, that is, a re-seller, hence, fairly defined as a merchant?

Problem 4.9

➤ What is the effect of a "conditioned sales contract?"

➤ Under § 2-402 it is treated as a reservation of a security interest, hence, making Article 9 relevant. Note that § 2-401 provides that title passes upon the completion of the sales transaction.

Problem 4.10

➤ Did title pass, that is, did the sale from Osterman to Pippin pass title?

➤ If so, in view of the bad check, does Osterman have any remedy?

➤ May Osterman repossess?

➤ May Osterman sue for replevin?

➤ Isn't there a failure of consideration?

➤ Do any of these remedies and contentions affect title?

Example and Questions

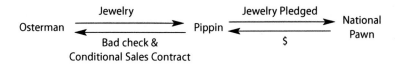

Questions

Problem 4.11

➤ Is National Pawn a good faith purchaser for value? Does that affect its rights?

Problem 4.12

➤ Could Osterman have protected itself?

➤ Has Osterman taken a PMSI in the Jewelry sold to Pippin?

➤ Could Osterman have filed a financing statement within 20 days of Pippin receiving possession, thereby perfecting Osterman's interest as of the date of the sale, based on the relation back effect? What U.C.C. Code section or sections apply?

➤ Does it make a difference if Pippin is a consumer buyer or a merchant buyer?

Problem 4.13

➤ Can National Pawn ever be sure that someone pledging collateral or for that matter selling their piece of personal property has clear title?

Problem 4.14

➤ What are the risks that a Pawn Shop or anyone loaning against a pledge takes? What would you, as a lawyer, advise your client, National Pawn to do?

Problem 4.15

➤ If National had voluntarily relinquished possession and Osterman had filed a UCC #1 during the interval between National giving up possession and then regaining possession, wouldn't Osterman's security interest have priority over National's regardless of other facts? What Code section applies?

➤ Using the diagram above, would it be different if National relinquished possession to the police as part of an official investigation?

For a discussion of what constitutes the debtor's rights in the collateral see Lawrence R. Ahern III, *The Law of Debtors and Creditors* § 7.66 (West 2011). Professor Ahern writes:

Article 9 does not delineate what degree of the debtor's interest in collateral is necessary to meet this requirement. Clearly if the debtor has outright ownership of collateral, the debtor has sufficient rights in the collateral. By the same token, mere possession of the goods is not sufficient. For example, if a debtor was merely holding goods as a bailee for a third party, the debtor would not have sufficient rights in the goods for attachment. The owner's consent can arise by way of estoppel if the owner of the collateral allows another to appear as the owner of the collateral or to dispose of the collateral such that a third party is led into dealing with the apparent owner as though it were the actual owner.

Comment 2 to § 9-203 provides:

6. *Debtor's Rights; Debtor's Power to Transfer Rights.* Subsection (b)(2) conditions attachment on the debtor's having "rights in the collateral or the power to transfer rights in the collateral to a secured party." A debtor's limited rights in collateral, short of full ownership, are sufficient for a security interest to attach. However, in accordance with basic personal property conveyancing principles, the baseline rule is that a security interest attaches only to whatever rights a debtor may have, broad or limited as those rights may be.

Certain exceptions to the baseline rule enable a debtor to transfer, and a security interest to attach to, greater rights than the debtor has. See Part 3, Subpart 3 (priority rules). The phrase, "or the power to transfer rights in the collateral to a secured party," accommodates those exceptions. In some cases, a debtor may have power to transfer another person's rights only to a class of transferees that excludes secured parties. *See*, e.g., Section 2-403(2) (giving certain merchants power to transfer an entruster's rights to a buyer in ordinary course of business). Under those circumstances, the debtor would not have the power to create a security interest in the other person's rights, and the condition in subsection (b)(2) would not be satisfied.

Also consider the law governing instruments as defined in Article 3 as to the ability of a holder of bearer paper, even if a thief, to transfer rights to the instrument to a holder in due course.

Thorp Credit, Inc. v. Wuchter

412 N.W.2d 641 (Ct. App. Iowa 1987)
(edited; citations omitted)

DONIELSON, Presiding Judge

The plaintiff, Thorp Credit, Inc., appeals the judgment of the district court that the defendants' son, Eric Wuchter, was the owner of certain cows and that those cows were not subject to Thorp's security interest against livestock owned by the defendants, Eugene and Louise Wuchter. Thorp on appeal contends that the trial court erred: (1) in finding that Eric Wuchter was the owner of the disputed cows; (2) in failing to find that the Wuchters were authorized to pledge Eric's cows as collateral for farm obligations allegedly based on the consolidation of the parties' farming operations; and (3) in failing to find that Eric was estopped from asserting ownership of the cows, where Eric allegedly clothed his father with the indicia of ownership, and where Eric's silence regarding his ownership of the disputed cows was allegedly relied upon by Thorp. We affirm.

In 1981 and 1982, the defendants, Eugene and Louise Wuchter, entered into loan agreements with the plaintiff, Thorp Credit, Inc., in which they borrowed $256,000.00 and $12,970.16. A security agreement dated August 26, 1981, granted Thorp a security interest in all the defendants' "livestock, milk cows, open and bred heifers, yearlings … whether now owned or hereafter acquired."

Following default by the Wuchters in repayment of the loans, Thorp obtained judgment in its favor. In May 1983 Thorp commenced a replevin action to recover all the cows on the Wuchters' farm. In June 1983 the Wuchters filed for bankruptcy. During the period of the bankruptcy, proceedings were stayed on the replevin action. Thorp sought relief from the stay in April 1985. When Thorp was finally ready and able to repossess the cows, the Wuchters' son, Eric, intervened in the action, claiming that he owned some of the cows and that those cows were not subject to Thorp's security interest.

* * *

The trial court found that Eric was the owner of the disputed cows and that those cows were not subject to the plaintiff's security interest. Thorp's motion for reconsideration was denied on December 10, 1985.

* * *

We first address Thorp's argument that the trial court erred in finding that Eric Wuchter owned the disputed cattle. Thorp contends that the defendant Eugene Wuchter held all the incidents of ownership in the disputed cows. Thorp argues that Eric's only claim to ownership is based solely on his name being listed on a registration form filed with the Holstein-Friesian Association located in Vermont. We disagree.

"Ownership" is a collection of rights to use and enjoy property, including the rights to sell and transmit it. 63 Am.Jur.2d *Property*, § 31 at 261 (1984). Ownership therefore consists of the possession of things, coupled with an unrestricted right of use, enjoyment, and disposal of such property, and is thus entitled to the property's products and profits. The term "owner," however, is of quite general application and is frequently applied to one having an interest in property less than absolute. The owner is also one who, in case of destruction of the property, must sustain the loss of it. 63 Am.Jur. *Property*, § 31 at 261 (1984).

A rebuttable presumption of ownership arises from the possession of property. One has possession of personal property when that property is held under that person's dominion and is subject to that person's control. Possession, however, is only one of the incidents of ownership of personalty, and one may have possession as an agent, or have possession merely as a custodian with consent of the owner.

* * *

The record reveals that most of the dairy cows claimed by Eric were registered with the Holstein-Friesian Association well before Thorp was granted a security interest in the defendants' livestock and therefore does not evidence an intent to mask the true ownership of the dairy cows. While the certificates of registration on their face state that the certificates do not guarantee actual ownership, we find that the filing dates indicate that it was the Wuchters' intent at the time of registration that Eric be considered the owner of the registered cows. We also note that all of Eric's livestock was registered, while Eugene Wuchter had not registered any of his cattle since 1972.

Upon examination of the record, we also agree with the trial court's conclusion that the farming operation of the Wuchters is not unique in today's farm economy. The record reveals that the money earned from the milk production from Eric's cows was combined with his father Eugene's receipts. Eric testified that this was done to cover the cost of feed for the cows and the rent on various pastures on which Eric's cows were kept. Any proceeds from the sale of cows or their offspring were placed back into the farm operation in order to cover the cost of Eric's cows' feed and board. In return for helping run the Wuchters' dairy operation, the defendant Eugene Wuchter paid Eric a monthly salary of $500.00.

The record also reveals that Eric's brother, Ed, borrowed money from various lending institutions in order to provide Eric the necessary financing to purchase additional dairy livestock. Eric testified that his father occasionally would purchase a cow for him, but that this sum would be deducted from his wages. Eric testified, however, that he did borrow money one time from the Farm Service Corporation, at which time Eric gave a purchase money security interest in his cows to Farm Service in order to purchase new cows.

* * *

Eric testified that on at least one occasion he specifically pointed out to the representatives from Thorp the cows in which he claimed ownership. Eric testified that he pointed out approximately fifteen head of dairy cows, the remaining cows resting in various pastures which Eric rented. Brad Knowler, a representative of Thorp, was also called to testify. Knowler testified that he had no knowledge that any of the cows were registered at the time he visited the Wuchter farm. Knowler additionally testified that no one ever stated to him that any of the cows belonged to Eric. On cross-examination, however, Knowler admitted that an appraisal sheet signed by his companion and bearing Knowler's name indicated that in March 1984 Eric had asserted to Knowler and his representative that he was the owner of some of the dairy cows in question. Knowler also admitted that the commercial loan officer at Thorp would have known about the registration of the disputed cows, but that there was nothing in the record showing any holstein registrations in any of the security agreements signed by the defendants Eugene and Louise Wuchter. Knowler admitted that there were no documents showing that Thorp had obtained security in any registered animals and stated that Thorp had made no claim to any registered animals. It is therefore apparent that Thorp was aware that Eric's registered cows were not covered in the security agreement, and it is also clear that Thorp was informed on at least one occasion that Eric claimed a number of the disputed cows.

Thorp also contends that the disputed cows were covered under the security agreement signed by the defendants Eugene and Louise Wuchter. The security agreement signed by Eugene and Louise Wuchter provides that Thorp shall have a security interest in all "farm products ... [including] livestock ... milk cows, open and bred heifers, yearlings ... now owned or hereafter acquired." Thorp argues that this blanket security agreement was sufficient to encompass all of the disputed cows claimed by Eric. Eric, however, argues that the security agreement was too general and did not specifically identify the registered dairy cows, rendering such cows outside the parameters of the security agreement.

* * *

In the present case, Brad Knowler testified that someone at Thorp would have known about the registration of holstein cows. Knowler, however, testified that Thorp undertook no specific identification of the nearly 350 head of dairy cows other than as to a broad number. Knowler additionally testified that they did not keep close tabs on the identity of the animals and did not undertake any identification procedures such as ear tag numbers.

While descriptions of collateral need not be painstakingly detailed or accurate, neither should such descriptions be loose or inaccurate. 69 Am.Jur.2d *Secured Transactions*, §292 at 126–27 (1973). In the present case, there was no description in the security agreement regarding those dairy cows that were registered. Testimony at trial revealed that loan officers at Thorp were aware that holstein dairy cows may be registered. The record also reveals that registered holstein dairy cows bring several hundred dollars more than unregistered cows. Eric testified that all of his registered cows were ear tagged. Brad Knowler testified that no methods of identification were utilized other than to generally count the number of head on the farm. Because the registered cattle were unique from those acknowledged as being owned by Eugene and Louise Wuchter, and because the security agreement contained no reference to these registered cows, we agree with the trial court's conclusion that the disputed cows were not subject to Thorp's security agreement.

Thorp, however, additionally points out that Eugene and Louise Wuchter signed a statement indicating that everything on the farm belonged to them. Thorp therefore argues that Eugene and Louise were authorized by Eric to pledge the cows as collateral for the farm operations. Thorp first argues that Eric clothed Eugene with authority to act as his agent and that Eugene had apparent authority to act on Eric's behalf regarding the disputed cows. Thorp argues in the alternative that Eric and Eugene in essence formed a partnership as a result of their combined efforts and that therefore Eugene's signature on the security agreement was binding on Eric.

We first address Thorp's argument that Eugene Wuchter was an agent of Eric and therefore had apparent authority to bind Eric to the security agreement. Though we find no express agreement between Eric and Eugene establishing an agency relationship, an agency relationship may be proven from the parties' words and conduct, from which an intention to create an agency may be implied. A fundamental principle of agency law is that whatever an agent does, within the scope of his actual authority, binds his principal. Actual authority to act is created when a principal intentionally confers authority on the agent either by writing or through other conduct which reasonably interpreted allows the agent to believe he has the power to act. Apparent authority to do acts or make contracts is that which, although not actually granted, has been knowingly permitted by the principal or which he holds the agent out as possessing. Thus, when apparent authority exists, the manifestations of the principal to another party to a transaction must be interpreted in light of what the other party knows or should know instead of what the agent knows or should know. But the principal must have acted in such a manner as to lead persons dealing with the agent to believe the agent has authority.

In the present case, Eric testified that he had permitted his father to receive Eric's portion of the milk receipts to pay feed expenses for the disputed cows and the rent for the various pastures rented by Eric. Eugene at various times also bought and sold registered cows on behalf of Eric. It is therefore apparent that Eric authorized Eugene to pay Eric's bills from the milk receipts and apply any of Eric's proceeds for other expenses incurred in raising the disputed cows. We do not, however, find any evidence that Eric clothed Eugene with any apparent authority to pledge his cows as security for Eugene's debts.

We initially note that Eugene and Louise were not acting on behalf of Eric when they took out the two loans from Thorp, but were acting on their own behalf. The intent is clear from the financing and security agreements that Eugene and Louise were to be solely responsible for the repayment of the loans. Though Eric would undoubtedly benefit from their influx of capital into the family's farm operations, such benefits were incidental to the taking of the loans. Moreover, we find no evidence of any occasion in which Eric authorized Eugene to pledge his cows as a security for any debts accumulated by Eugene. The record reveals that on the one occasion that Eric borrowed money for the purchase of new livestock, it was Eric himself who pledged several of his cows as a security interest. Assuming that some form of agency relationship existed between Eric and Eugene, we do not believe that the granting of permission by Eric for Eugene to receive Eric's milk receipts to apply to Eric's bills regarding the feed and rent translates into authority in Eugene to pledge as security dairy cows which are not owned by him. We thus find no evidence that Eric conferred authority on Eugene to pledge Eric's cattle as security for loans for which Eric was not liable, nor do we believe that Eric's conduct could have created a reasonable belief by Thorp that Eugene had the authority to pledge Eric's cows as security. While Eugene's and Louise's actions may have misled Thorp, we cannot say that Eric's actions resulted in Thorp believing that Eugene and Louise were authorized to pledge Eric's cows.

Thorp additionally argues that, assuming the trial court is correct in its characterization of a family farming operation, it is clear that the relationship between Eugene and Eric was a joint venture or partnership. Consequently, Thorp contends that because a partner is authorized to act on behalf of the partnership, Eugene's signature on Thorp's security agreement is binding on the partnership, including Eric. We disagree.

A partnership is defined as "an association of two or more persons to carry on as co-owners a business for profit." Four elements are necessary to create a partnership: (1) an intent by the parties to associate as partners; (2) a business; (3) earning of profits; and (4) co-ownership of profits, property, and control. Under Iowa law, an intention to associate is the crucial test of a partnership. An intention to associate need not be in writing; an intent to associate may be gleaned from the conduct of the parties and the circumstances surrounding the transactions.

Upon a thorough examination of the record in the present case, we find that no partnership was created as between Eric and Eugene. The record reveals that both Eric's and Eugene's dairy cows were combined into a single operation. The record also reveals that Eugene was the primary manager of the daily operations of the farm. Eric provided services as a laborer, for which Eugene paid Eric approximately $500.00 per month. The milk proceeds from the cows were commingled, only one milk check being sent to the parties. No attempt was made to determine what feed and milk Eric's cows used and produced as opposed to Eugene's cows.

The record also reveals, however, that Eugene would deduct from Eric's wages the price of a new head of livestock which he purchased on Eric's behalf. Eric testified that his father considered him an employee of the farm. No partnership tax returns were filed; rather, Eugene claimed the proceeds from the dairy operations as income on his personal tax returns. There is no evidence in the record that Eric was held out as co-owner of the assets of the farm or in fact had any interest in the operation other than in his own dairy cows. Concerning the buying and selling of the operation's dairy cows, there is no evidence in the record to support a finding that Eric had any authority to buy or sell any cows other than those which he personally bought or sold. The record reveals that there was no attempt to divide the profits from the milk receipts equally between Eric and Eugene; all proceeds were given to Eugene. The record does not reveal that a joint bank account was opened whereby both Eric and Eugene would be authorized to pay expenses and deposit receipts.

From these facts we conclude that no partnership existed as between Eric and Eugene. Even assuming, *arguendo*, that Eric and Eugene had a joint interest in the dairy cattle, such a fact does not of itself establish that a partnership existed. Additionally, the sharing of gross returns does not of itself establish a partnership whether or not the persons sharing them have a joint or common right or interest in any property from which the returns were derived. While the receipt by a person of the share of the profits of a business is prima-facie evidence that the person is a partner in the business, no such inference may be drawn if such profits were received in payment as wages of an employee. In the present case Eric received $500.00 per month in wages as an employee. We thus find no evidence of a partnership and therefore hold that the disputed dairy cows were owned by Eric and that as such they were not subject to Thorp's security agreement.

Thorp lastly argues that even if the trial court was correct in concluding that Eric was the owner of the disputed cows, Eric should be estopped from denying the validity of Thorp's security interest based on Eric's alleged silence regarding ownership. Based upon the above discussion and examination of the various other arguments raised by Thorp, we find no merit in this argument.

AFFIRMED.

Questions

Problem 4.16

➣ What do you think of the court's discussion of Iowa farming operations?

➣ In other words, what is that discussion's significance?

Problem 4.17

➣ What are the indicia of ownership by the defendants that Thorp claimed it relied on?

Problem 4.18

➣ In rejecting Thorp's argument, what did the court hold with reference to Article 9 perfection?

Problem 4.19

➣ Despite the bankruptcy filing by the defendants and the automatic stay, the court states "[w]hen Thorp was finally ready and able to repossess the cows...." What made Thorp *able* to repossess?

Discussion

ENTRUSTING TO A MERCHANT (§ 2-403) AND ARTICLE 9

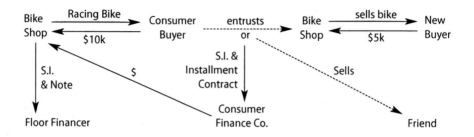

Floor Planner has an inventory security interest, which floats over inventory held for sale. It is released on any item sold to a BIOC. *See,* § 9-320(a). It does not reattach if goods are merely entrusted to the merchant rather than returned.

The grant of security interest is in the security agreement. Together a security agreement or lease agreement or conditional sale agreement *and* monetary obligation constitute chattel paper.

The Consumer Finance Co. is automatically perfected upon attachment of the security interest, since the Consumer Finance Company took a PMSI in consumer goods. *See,* § 9-309(1).

Friend purchases the bike from the Consumer Buyer free of the security interest of the Consumer Finance Company, if the Consumer Finance Company did not "super perfect" and the Friend purchased the bike in good faith and for personal or family use, keeping the Bike as a consumer good. Perfection automatically occurs; however, super perfection of a consumer good occurs by filing. If Consumer Finance Company super perfected, the Friend takes the Bike subject to Consumer Finance Company's security interest. *See,* § 9-320(b).

If the Consumer Buyer entrusts the bike to the Bike Shop for repair or maintenance, and the Bike Shop sells the bike to a New Buyer, committing fraud, the New Buyer gets all of the entrusting person's rights in the goods. If the New Buyer is a BIOC, then § 2-403(2) applies. In this example, the Consumer Buyer had encumbered title; therefore, the New Buyer will also get an encumbered title. Note that § 2-403(2) is an exception to the principle of derivative title, which holds that a transferor can only transfer the rights it has.

C. Methods of Perfection and Priority Arising Therefrom

1. Automatic

Automatic perfection occurs upon attachment. *See* § 9-309.

Questions

Problem 4.20

➢ What is the reason behind the automatic perfection of PMSIs in consumer goods?

➢ The chief exception under § 9-311 is for automobiles.

Problem 4.21

➢ Why the distinction between a PMSI in consumer goods and a non-purchase money security interest in consumer goods?

Problem 4.22

➢ Look at § 9-309 (2), (3), and (4). What is the reasoning behind allowing automatic perfection? *See also*, § 9-109(4)-(7) (excluding certain transactions from the scope of Article 9).

Note that in Georgia, § 9-309(14) does not apply. In Georgia a winner of the lottery who opts for a payout based on a present value analysis cannot cash it out later on.

2. Filing a Financing Statement

Another way for a security interest to be perfected is filing a financing statement, also known as a UCC #1. *See*, § 9-521 (providing a sample form). *See also*, § 9-310. In Georgia, the U.C.C. checklists, U.C.C. forms, and Administrative Procedures are located on the Georgia Superior Clerks' Cooperative Authority website at:

http://www.gsccca.org/filesandforms/uccforms.asp

Questions

Problem 4.23

➢ Consider again the classification of collateral as tangible, quasi-tangible, intangible, or other. Which of these forms of collateral *must* be perfected by filing when used as commercial financing security?

➢ Which forms of collateral *may* be perfected by filing?

Problem 4.24

➢ Which of the above are *most likely* to constitute proceeds from the sale of other collateral?

Problem 4.25

➢ Which of the above, although perfected as proceeds, may lose their priority status to a purchaser giving new value in the ordinary course of the purchaser's business?

3. Pursuant to Non-Code Statutes or Regulations

A third method of perfecting a security interest is pursuant to non-code statutes or regulations. *See*, §9-311.

Questions

Problem 4.26

➢ Why the exception in §9-311(d)?

Problem 4.27

➢ If the Debtor moves to State B from State A with his automobile and gets a clean certificate of title issued, that is, one without the "lien" in favor of a secured creditor noted on the original certificate issued by State A, what should the secured party do? *See*, Comment 7 to §9-311.

4. By Filing, Possession, or Control

Certain collateral may be perfected by filing, possession, or control. *See*, §9-312. In analyzing §9-312, a distinction must be made between personal property used as original collateral and that same property that comprises proceeds of the originally perfected collateral. Under §9-315(a)(2), a "security interest attaches to any identifiable proceeds of collateral." Under §9-315(c), that security interest is perfected "if the security interest in the original collateral was perfected."

Questions

Problem 4.28

➢ Section 9-312(a) provides for permissive perfection by filing. Note that the listed collateral may be original collateral (for example, in-

vestment property) or either original collateral or proceeds of original collateral. What method of perfection would you advise your client
to use if the listed collateral was original collateral? Explain.

Problem 4.29

➢ Section 9-312(b)(1) and (3) provides that if used as original collateral a deposit account or money may only be perfected by control or
possession, respectively. Explain the reason behind this.

Problem 4.30

➢ Why is there a different rule for deposit accounts and money if they
are proceeds? *See*, § 9-315(b), (c), and (d).

➢ If proceeds, does the perfection under § 9-315(b), (c), and (d) protect
a secured party as well as perfection under § 9-312(b)(1) and (3)?

Example and Questions

Electronics, Inc., a retailer sells a 56-inch LCD television on credit to a Buyer
who buys the television for his family's personal use. In exchange, Electronics,
Inc. arranges financing through its affiliated Finance Company. Buyer signs a
security agreement and promissory note and takes possession of the television.

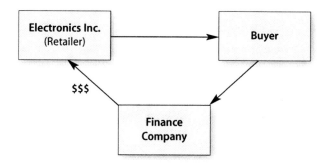

Questions

Problem 4.31

➢ Does the Finance Company have a PMSI in the television? Explain.

➢ What is the difference between a PMSI and non-purchase money security interest?

Problem 4.32

➢ What value has the buyer received from the Finance Company?

Problem 4.33

➤ Does the Finance Company need to file a UCC #1 to perfect its interest?

➤ What protection does the Finance Company get if it files a UCC #1?

Problem 4.34

➤ If the Buyer is sued and a judgment against him is enforced, will a Judgment Creditor's lien interest prime the interest of the Finance Company assuming the Judgment Creditor attempts an execution? *See,* §9-317(a)(2).

Problem 4.35

➤ If the Buyer files a Chapter 7 Bankruptcy case, will the Finance Company or the Chapter 7 Bankruptcy Trustee have priority to the television set, assuming the Buyer, now a Debtor under the bankruptcy code, does not claim the television as exempt property? *See,* §9-320.

Problem 4.36

➤ If the Debtor claims the television as exempt, does Finance Company lose its security interest? *See,* Bankruptcy Code §522(f)(2).

Bankruptcy Code §522(f) provides the Federal bankruptcy exemptions that a debtor may claim. *See,* O.C.G.A. §44-13-100(b) for Georgia bankruptcy exemptions. A distinction is made between a PMSI and a non-purchase money interest or judgment lien by allowing a debtor to "avoid" the fixing of a judicial lien except "for a domestic support obligation" (child and spousal support), or a non possessory, non-purchase-money security interest in any "consumer goods, tools of trade, or prescribed health aids" that impair an exemption. *See,* Bankruptcy Code §§522(f)(1)(A) and (B) and 523(a)(5).

Problem 4.37

➤ If the Buyer had sold the television to his next door neighbor for $1,000 two months after his purchase of it, and then filed for bankruptcy some time later, which party would prevail in a contest over the television set: (a) the Neighbor, (b) the Finance Company, or (c) the Trustee? *See,* §9-320 and Bankruptcy Code §§544(b), 548(a), and 550(b).

In re Honcoop

377 B.R. 719 (Bankr. M.D. Fla., 2007)
(edited; citations omitted)

FUNK, Bankruptcy Judge

This Case is before the Court upon [Chapter 13] Debtor's Motion to Value Claim Four (4) of Nicholas Financial, Inc. After a hearing held on July 18, 2007, the Court makes the following Findings of Fact and Conclusions of Law.

FINDINGS OF FACT

* * *

On October 26, 2004, less than 910 days prior to filing her case, Debtor purchased a 1999 Mercury Mountaineer for $12,000. Debtor financed the vehicle through a Simple Finance Contract that was assigned to Nicholas Financial Inc. ("Creditor"). In conjunction with the purchase of the vehicle, Debtor was charged $500.00 for GAP insurance, which was added to the purchase price. The total amount of the contract came to $11,339.90, for a period of forty-eight (48) months with an APR of 19.25%. The contract did not allocate the monthly payments of $343.11 between the purchase price and GAP insurance.

On May 1, 2007, Creditor filed a Proof of Claim in the amount of $11,499.00. Debtor subsequently filed a Motion to Value Creditor's Claim Four (4), in which she alleged that the vehicle had a replacement value of $4,570.00. On June 6, 2007, Creditor filed an Objection to Debtor's Motion to Value upon the basis that pursuant to the hanging paragraph of 11 U.S.C. § 1325(a), Debtor was not entitled to value her vehicle for an amount less than what was owed under the contract price.

CONCLUSIONS OF LAW

Prior to the adoption of BAPCPA, a debtor could bifurcate a motor vehicle secured loan into secured and unsecured components, treating the claim as secured up to the extent of the vehicle's value and unsecured for the remainder. BAPCPA, which took effect on October 17, 2005, added a provision to 11 U.S.C. § 1325(a) commonly referred to as the "hanging paragraph." The hanging paragraph provides in pertinent part:

> "For purposes of paragraph (5), section 506 shall not apply to a claim described in that paragraph if the creditor has a purchase money security interest securing the debt that is the subject of the claim, the debt

was incurred within the 910-day preceding the date of the filing of the pe-
tition, and the collateral for that debt consists of a motor vehicle ... ac-
quired for the personal use of the debtor ..."

In the instant case, there is no dispute that: 1) the collateral for the debt is a
motor vehicle; 2) the vehicle was purchased within 910 days preceding the filing of Debtor's bankruptcy petition; and 3) Debtor acquired the vehicle for
personal use. The contested issue is whether Creditor has a purchase money security interest in the vehicle.

Debtor argues that the inclusion of the GAP insurance premium into the Simple Finance Contract destroys Creditor's purchase money security interest. As
a result, Debtor argues that the hanging paragraph does not apply and she can
therefore bifurcate her claim into secured and unsecured parts pursuant to 11
U.S.C. §506(a)(1). Creditor argues that it has a purchase money security interest in the Vehicle notwithstanding the inclusion of the GAP insurance being
financed into the purchase price.

Whether a creditor has a purchase money security interest is determined by
looking to state law.

* * *

A bankruptcy court in Georgia held that payment of an extended service
contract, documentary fee and certificate of title fee were to be considered part
of the purchase price of the vehicle, due to the relationship between those
items and the vehicle. *In re Murray*, 352 B.R. [340, 349 (Bankr. M.D. Ga.
2006)]. The Court notes however that GAP insurance was not one of the items
considered by the Court in *Murray*.

* * *

Accordingly, the Court must determine whether GAP insurance is part of
the "price" of the vehicle or whether it was "value given to enable [Debtor] to
acquire rights in the collateral." The Court finds guidance in Comment 3 to
the Uniform Commercial Code which provides that "the 'price' of collateral or
the 'value given to enable' includes obligations incurred in connection with acquiring rights in the collateral ... The concept of 'purchase money security interest' requires a close nexus between the acquisition of the collateral and a
secured obligation...."

Thus, the Court will address the extent to which a nonessential item, such
as GAP insurance, may properly be construed as part of the purchase price.
The Court finds that it is only proper to include those nonessential items that

enhance or improve the value of the vehicle, such as window tinting or undercoating, in the purchase price. Clearly GAP insurance does not fit into this category, as the sole purpose of GAP insurance is to protect the owner of the vehicle in instances in which the portion of damage done to the vehicle is greater than its value. As the very nature of GAP insurance does not involve the overall enhancement of the vehicle, it cannot be properly construed as part of the purchase price nor does the Court find the requisite close nexus between the inclusion of GAP insurance and the acquisition of the vehicle.

Having found that Debtor's obligation to Creditor is partially a purchase money security interest and partially a non purchase money security interest, the Court must determine the extent of Creditor's purchase money security interest by applying either the dual status or the transformation rule. The dual status rule provides that the secured lender has a purchase money security interest to the extent that the amount financed relates to the purchase price. However, under the transformation rule the secured creditor is deemed not to possess a purchase money security interest as the non-purchase money component transforms the entire claim into a non-purchase money security interest. *Id.*

In *Southtrust Bank of Alabama Nat'l Ass'n v. Borg-Warner Acceptance Corp.*, 760 F.2d 1240, 1242–43 (11th Cir.1985) the Eleventh Circuit Court of Appeals adopted the transformation rule. The court stated "[w]ithout some guidelines, legislative or contractual, the court should not be required to distill from a mass of transactions the extent to which a security interest is purchase money. Unless a lender contractually provides some method for determining the extent to which each item of collateral secures its purchase money, it effectively gives up its purchase money status." *Id.* at 1243.

Creditor asserts that the law has changed since the Eleventh Circuit's analysis and that the Court has the discretion as to whether to apply the dual status rule or the transformation rule to a partial purchase money security interest. Paragraphs 6 and 7 of Fla. Stat. §679.1031 provide:

> (6) A purchase-money security interest does not lose its status as such, even if:
>
>> (a) The purchase-money collateral also secures an obligation that is not a purchase-money obligation;
>>
>> (b) Collateral that is not purchase-money collateral also secures the purchase-money obligation; or
>>
>> (c) The purchase-money obligation has been renewed, refinanced, consolidated, or restructured.

(7) A secured party claiming a purchase-money security interest has the burden of establishing the extent to which the security interest is a purchase-money security interest.

The Court agrees that it has the discretion as to whether to apply the dual status or the transformation rule to a partial purchase money security interest and finds that with respect to GAP insurance, the equitable rule to be applied is the dual status rule. However, because the contract failed to allocate the portion of the monthly payments attributable to GAP insurance and the portion attributable to the vehicle itself, the Court finds it appropriate to remove the GAP insurance in its entirety. Accordingly, Creditor's secured claim will be reduced by $500.00, the amount of the GAP insurance. However, the remainder of Claim 4 is a purchase money security interest, is subject to §1325(a) and is not permitted to be bifurcated into secured and unsecured parts pursuant to 11 U.S.C. §506(a)(1).

CONCLUSION

Although GAP insurance is not part of the purchase price of a vehicle, the dual status rule is the appropriate rule to be applied. The Creditor's secured claim is due to be reduced by the amount of the GAP insurance. The remainder of Creditor's claim is a purchase money security interest, is subject to §1325(a) and is not permitted to be bifurcated into secured and unsecured parts pursuant to 11 U.S.C. §506(a)(1). A separate order consistent with these Findings of Fact and Conclusions of will be entered.

Discussion

Courts that rely on §9-107's phrase "to the extent" follow the "dual status" rule. That rule provides that a security interest may be partially purchase-money and partially non-purchase money. Additionally, refinancing or consolidation with other debt does not automatically destroy the purchase money aspect of the security interest. See, *In re Lee*, 169 B.R. 790 (Bankr. S.D. Ga. 1994). Other Courts follow the transformation rule, as does *Southtrust Bank*. But see, §9-103.

Questions

Problem 4.38

➤ How might a Creditor successfully argue that the dual status rather than the transformation rule should apply? Is there an applicable Code section? If so cite it.

Problem 4.39

➤ Unlike the "dual status" rule, the transformation rule creates a novation. What is a novation?

Design Engineering, Construction International Inc. v. Cessna Finance Corporation

164 Ga. App. 159 (Ct. App. Ga. 1982)
(edited; code references updated; citations omitted)

CARLEY, Judge

The facts, insofar as they are relevant to the instant appeal, are as follows: Appellant-plaintiff, Design Engineering, Construction International Inc. (DECI), purchased an airplane from Outlaw Aircraft Sales Inc. (Outlaw). The sale was evidenced by a conditional sales contract financing the unpaid balance of the purchase price. The contract contained the following provision: "This contract may be assigned by the Seller [Outlaw] and, if so assigned, the assignee shall have and be entitled to exercise any and all rights and powers of the Seller hereunder and all obligations and duties of the Buyer [DECI] to or for the Seller shall be obligations and duties to or for such assignee and when so assigned the contract shall be free from any claims whatsoever which Buyer may have against Seller. All payments or other moneys due hereunder and under the Note secured hereby shall be paid by Buyer to such assignee without recoupment, set-off or counterclaim, either in law or in equity." In addition to the conditional sales contract and, as part of the same transaction, DECI executed a promissory note to Outlaw for the unpaid balance of the purchase price of the airplane. On the same day that DECI purchased the airplane, Outlaw, for value received, assigned the conditional sales contract and endorsed the promissory note to appellee-defendant, Cessna Finance Corporation (CFC).

DECI subsequently defaulted on the underlying conditional sales contract and the note. DECI then instituted the instant action against Outlaw, Cessna Aircraft Company and appellee-CFC. As against CFC, the complaint alleged a claim for the breach of implied warranties of merchantability and fitness for a particular purpose in connection with the aircraft DECI had purchased from Outlaw. DECI also sought, pursuant to [§ 2-609], rescission of the underlying "agreements, contracts and notes" on the basis that CFC had repudiated those agreements through its failure, after demand, to give "adequate assurance of due performance" of the implied and express warranties on the airplane.

In its answer, CFC denied the material allegations of the complaint. CFC also filed a counterclaim seeking to recover on the conditional sales contract and the promissory note which had been assigned and endorsed to it by Outlaw, the seller. After extensive discovery, CFC moved for summary judgment in the main action and on its counterclaim. The trial court granted CFC's motion in its entirety. It is from this order that DECI brings the instant appeal.

We turn first to the grant of summary judgment to CFC on its counterclaim. The relevant statute with reference to the assigned conditional sales contract is [§9-403]: "Subject to any statute or decision which establishes a different rule for buyers of consumer goods, an agreement by a buyer that he will not assert against an assignee any claim or defense which he may have against the seller is enforceable by an assignee who takes his assignment for value, in good faith and without notice of a claim or defense, except as to defenses of a type which may be asserted against a holder in due course of a negotiable instrument under the Article on Commercial Paper (Article 3) [§9-403]. A buyer who as part of one transaction signs both a negotiable instrument and a security agreement makes such an agreement." The relevant statute with reference to the promissory note, [§3-302(a)(ii)], provides: "A holder in due course is a holder who takes the instrument (a) for value; and (b) in good faith; and (c) without notice that it is overdue or has been dishonored or of any defense against it or claim to it on the part of any person."

DECI apparently concedes that the defenses that it seeks to assert against enforcement of the conditional sales contract and the note would not be assertable against one having holder in due course status. [See §3-305.] DECI states in its brief that "[t]he consideration of this appeal boils down to a single issue. Is the 'Party-to-the-transaction Rule' a viable legal concept under Georgia law or not." The "party-to-the-transaction rule" is a legal principle in the law of negotiable instruments and has been adopted in several jurisdictions. That legal principle establishes, in effect, a defense to the assertion of holder in due course status. As stated by the Supreme Court of New Jersey, the premise upon which the "rule" is based is that "[i]n the field of negotiable instruments, good faith is a broad concept. The basic philosophy of the holder in due course status is to encourage free negotiability of commercial paper by removing certain anxieties of one who takes the paper as an innocent purchaser knowing no reason why the paper is not as sound as its face would indicate. It would seem to follow, therefore that the more the holder knows about the underlying transaction, and particularly the more he controls or participates or becomes involved in it, the less he fits the role of a good faith purchaser for value; the closer his relationship to the underlying agreement which is the source of the note, the less need there is for giving him the tension-free rights considered necessary in a fast-moving, credit extending commercial world." While the conditional sales contract is not a negotiable instrument, DECI asserts that the same rationale of the "party-to-the-transaction" rule would attach because, under [§ 9-403], the assignee must take his assignment in "good faith" and "without notice of a claim or defense", conditions which, according to DECI, cannot be demonstrated if the assignee was, in effect, a "party to the transaction."

Our independent research confirms that the "party-to-the-transaction rule" has apparently never been directly addressed by the appellate courts of this state. However, our review of the record in the instant case also demonstrates that, in resolving the issues raised in this appeal, we need not make a definitive decision as to whether that legal principle is or is not viable in Georgia. This is true because, even when viewed in light of the foreign authorities enunciating and adopting the "rule," the evidence in the instant case, contrary to DECI's assertions, would not support a finding that CFC, the assignee of the contract and note, was an "original party" to the underlying sale. Outlaw, the seller, is a wholly independent dealer and is not owned or controlled by CFC. The fact that CFC prescribed the forms and documents to be used by Outlaw when financing a sale through it and specified the terms and conditions upon which it would accept them does not demonstrate that CFC was the "original creditor." Apparently, Outlaw was free to finance through companies other than CFC. Accordingly, even assuming that the "party-to-the-transaction" rule were viable in Georgia, it is clear that the evidence in the instant case fails to demonstrate that CFC's counterclaim would come within it.

The evidence demonstrates that CFC took the conditional sales contract and the note for value, in good faith and without notice of any defense or claim to them on the part of any person. DECI has presented no credible evidence to the contrary and has raised no defenses assertable against one otherwise entitled to claim holder in due course status. Accordingly, we find no error in the grant of summary judgment in favor of CFC on its counterclaim against DECI.

We turn now to the grant of summary judgment to CFC on the main action. As to the breach of warranty claim, CFC was the mere assignee of the contract and note, was not the seller of the airplane and, for the reasons discussed in Division 1, was not a "party" to the sale. There is simply no basis for asserting a breach of warranty claim against CFC and it was not error to grant summary judgment in favor of CFC as to this count of the complaint. Likewise, with regard to the count premised upon the provisions of [§ 2-609], CFC was not a "party" to the underlying contract for sale of the airplane and the statute is simply inapplicable insofar as a potential claim by DECI against CFC is concerned. CFC has holder in due course status and the claims which DECI seeks to assert in the main action against CFC are simply not assertable against one having such status. Cf. [§ 3-305]. DECI's contractual remedies based upon the breach of duties arising from the underlying sale of the airplane must be asserted against those parties to the transaction upon whom these duties are imposed.

Questions

Problem 4.40

➤ In a conditional sales contract, what is Outlaw, the supplier of goods, attempting to do?

Problem 4.41

➤ Is a conditional sales contract subject to Article 9, that is, is it a security agreement for Article 9 purposes?

Problem 4.42

➤ Which party has title to the goods, DECI or Outlaw? *See*, §2-401(1).

Problem 4.43

➤ What served as the collateral for the monetary obligation created by the promissory note?

Problem 4.44

➤ When Outlaw assigned the conditional sales contract and endorsed the promissory note to CFC, who then had a right to foreclose on the collateral if the monetary obligation was not paid?

Problem 4.45

➤ CFC claimed holder in due course ("HDC") status. What does it mean to be a HDC?

➤ How does a party perfect its security interest in a negotiable note?

Problem 4.46

➤ If DECI prevails on its warranty claims, does it still have to pay CFC? Explain. In this regard note that the party to the transaction rule is akin to the close connectedness doctrine.

Discussion

The close-connectedness doctrine is a judicially created doctrine protective of a consumer buyer's or lessee's rights in certain credit transactions. The doctrine effectively denies a holder in due course status to an assignee of a negotiable note if the assignee is too closely related to the seller or supplier of the goods. Evidence of close-connectedness include:

(1) Drafting by the transferee of forms for the transferor; (2) approval or establishment or both of the transferor's procedures by the transferee; (3) an independent check by the transferee on the credit of the debtor or some other direct contact between the transferee and the debtor; (4) heavy reliance by the transferor upon the transferee (e.g., transfer by the transferor of all or substantial part of his paper to the transferee) and ; (5) common or connected ownership or management of the transferor and transferee. *See, Vitols v. Citizens Banking Co.*, 10 F.3d 1227 (6th Cir. Ohio 1993).

In short, the close-connectedness doctrine preserves a buyer's or lessee's contract defenses to payment by a seller or supplier's breach against the holder of the instrument who would otherwise be entitled to payment.

The Federal Trade Commission, by regulations, mandates the following legend on negotiable notes signed by consumers:

Any holder of this Consumer Credit Contract are subject to all claims and defenses which the Debtor could assert against the seller of goods or services obtained [pursuant hereto or] with the proceeds hereof. Recovery hereunder by the Debtor shall not exceed amounts paid by the Debtor hereunder. *See,* 16 C.F.R. §433.2(a), (b).

D. Automatic Attachment— §9-203(f) through (i)

These provisions relate to the transfer or assignment of interests that are supported by underlying collateral in which a party already has a security interest. *See,* Comments 8, 9, and 10 to §9-203. Examples include: suretyship obligations and pledges of securities, and creation of a security interest in a brokerage account. *See also,* §§9-308(d), (e), (f), and (g).

E. U.C.C. §§9-315, 9-317, and 9-322

1. General Rules

Sections 9-315, 9-317, and 9-322 deal generally with priorities among and between secured creditors other than the rules applicable to PMSIs.

The first to perfect secures his interest regardless of which competing creditor first gives value. Article 9 has a *notice* filing system. Note that there is no perfection absent attachment, but once attachment occurs, perfection will relate back to an earlier filing of a financing statement. *See*, §§ 9-502(d) and 9-308(a).

Perfection for collateral perfects also to proceeds and other supporting obligations, for example, guarantees. Section 9-315(b)(2) deals with comingled cash proceeds and provides for tracing. Both *Shelby County State Bank v. Van Diest Supply Co.*, 303 F.3d 832 (7th Cir. 2002) and *Van Diest Supply Co. v. Shelby County State Bank*, 425 F.3d 437 (7th Cir. 2005) deal with priority and proceeds tracing issues. Excerpts from both cases follow along with pertinent questions.

Example and Questions

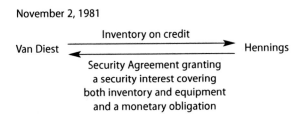

November 2, 1981

A financing statement entered into by Hennings and Van Diest on November 2, 1981, provided for a security interest in "[a]ll inventory, notes and accounts receivable, machinery and equipment now owned or hereafter acquired, including all replacements, substitutions and additions thereto."

Question

Problem 4.47

➤ The court refers to the grant of a security interest by Hennings as a "blanket lien." Does that terminology comport with Article 9?

On August 29, 1983, Hennings and Van Diest entered into a new security agreement ("the Security Agreement") the language of which is at the core of this dispute. The Security Agreement was based on a preprinted standard "Business Security Agreement" form. In the field for the description of collateral, the parties entered the following language, drafted by Van Diest, describing the security interest as being in

[a]ll inventory, including but not limited to agricultural chemicals, fertilizers, and fertilizer materials sold to Debtor by Van Diest Supply

Co. whether now owned or hereafter acquired, including all replacements, substitutions and additions thereto, and the accounts, notes,
and any other proceeds there from.

The Security Agreement contained a further preprinted clause providing

as additional collateral all additions to and replacements of all such
collateral and all accessories, accessions, parts and equipment now or
hereafter affixed thereto or used in connection with and the proceeds
from all such collateral (including negotiable or non-negotiable ware-
house receipts now or hereafter issued for storage of collateral).

Questions

Problem 4.48

➤ Does Van Diest need to file a new financing statement, that is, a new
UCC #1, to perfect its interest every time it enters into a new security
agreement?

Problem 4.49

➤ Why was a new security agreement entered into? Was the security interest a PMSI? Explain.

Problem 4.50

➤ A financing statement gives third parties *notice* that a party may have
a security interest. *See*, Part 5 of Article 9 dealing with the sufficiency
of a financing statement. Generally, the notice is referred to as "notice
to the world." Why is this important for the secured party and third
parties?

Problem 4.51

➤ If the financing statement covers all inventory and equipment but the
security agreement only covers inventory, what interest of the creditor is perfected?

Problem 4.52

➤ In the matter being discussed, are the financing statement and the security agreement consistent as to collateral coverage? Note that courts
treat the interpretation of contract as a question of law. In *Shelby*, 303
F.3d at 835, 836 the court stated:

> The description of the security interest in this case is a text-
> book example of ambiguous language: a term (all inventory)
> is followed by a qualifier (including all ...) and then another (sold

to Debtor by Van Diest). It is a basic rule of English syntax (of all syntax, in fact) that a modifier should be placed directly next to the element it aims to modify: placing two modifiers in a row leads to the question whether the latter one modifies only the first modifier, or modifies the entire term. In the first edition of his book on statutory interpretation, Sutherland described the "doctrine of the last antecedent" as providing that "[r]elative and qualifying phrases, grammatically and legally, where no contrary intention appears, refer solely to the last antecedent." J.G. Sutherland, Statutes and Statutory Construction § 267, at 349 (1st ed. 1891).

➤ What is the ambiguity?

➤ Is it helpful to know that Van Diest drafted the clause?

➤ Could parol evidence be admissible?

Example and Questions

In December of 1997 the following occurred:

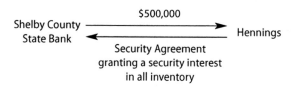

Shelby County State Bank properly perfected by filing a UCC #1. Shortly thereafter in April of 1998, Shelby County State Bank established a revolving credit in Hennings favor for $4 million.

Questions

Problem 4.53

➤ Would the security agreement of December 1997 cover both the 1997 and 1998 transactions?

Problem 4.54

➤ Does the 1997 perfection perfect the Bank's interest in the after-acquired inventory of Hennings?

➤ What is a revolving line of credit? *See*, § 9-204, "after-acquired property; future advances."

Problem 4.55

➤ Is Van Diest's UCC #1 filing still effective?

➤ If the answer is yes, why so, since financing statements are only effective for five years? *See*, §§ 9-515(a) and (d).

➤ At what time must a secured party re-file to ensure it is still properly perfected? *See*, § 9-322.

Example and Question

The court in *Van Diest*, 425 F.3d 439 stated:

> Van Diest held a perfected, first priority purchase money security interest in the inventory it sold to Hennings. Shelby, also a secured party, claimed a security interest in all inventory, accounts receivable, and equipment of Hennings. Van Diest contends that Shelby converted its property when Shelby received the proceeds from the sale of inventory Van Diest had supplied to Hennings. Van Diest does not challenge the district court's finding that the funds Hennings paid to Shelby directly by check written on Hennings's bank accounts are not at issue. Still at issue, though, are the direct payments to Shelby from Hennings's customers which did not pass through Hennings's bank account. After Hennings drew on the Note, and Shelby received accounts, Hennings customers either paid Shelby directly or wrote checks to Hennings, which Hennings delivered to Shelby. Van Diest contends it can show that each of these payments came from the sale of its collateral by showing the proportion of Hennings's inventory on the date of each transaction that was attributable to product that Van Diest had provided to Hennings.

The proceeds from the sale of both the inventory supplied by Van Diest and the inventory bought with the Bank's funds under the revolving credit have been commingled.

Question

Problem 4.56

➤ Does § 9-315(b)(2) help Van Diest? Explain.

Discussion

Note that a PMSI that is properly perfected (for example, with notice to previously perfected inventory financer) will prime (or be promoted over) the first filed creditor as to the specific collateral covered by the PMSI and the proceeds thereof unless the proceeds are a deposit account under the control of a competing secured party. *See* § 9-104 (providing the definition of control). A bank in control of a deposit account, that is, where the debtor maintains the depository account, has priority over a conflicting interest unless the conflicting secured party has become the bank's customer, such as through the establishment of a lock box.

2. Special Rules

Non-filing collateral: This is collateral including quasi-tangible collateral, where possession or control may result with the creditor in possession or control priming a previously perfected interest. This collateral includes deposit accounts,[1] investment property,[2] letter of credit rights,[3] and purchases of chattel paper and negotiable instruments.[4]

If the chattel paper is claimed as proceeds by the first perfected secured party, the inventory financer, and is then taken in the ordinary course of a financing creditor's business and the chattel paper does not indicate on its face that it may not be assigned, the financing creditor who is giving new value will prime the perfected inventory financer.

If the chattel paper is original collateral, then a second secured party giving value in the ordinary course of business without actual knowledge that he is violating the rights of the first perfected secured creditor (original filer) primes the first secured creditor if he gets possession or control. Good faith does not require a record search. Without more, a purchaser of chattel paper who has seen a financing statement covering the chattel paper or who knows that the chattel paper is encumbered, does not have knowledge that its purchase violates the secured party's rights.

Chattel paper, unlike accounts receivable includes a document signed by the debtor, hence, the debtor's obligation has a recognizable physical manifestation. The rule still applies whether the monetary obligation is a negotiable or non-negotiable note.

Note that § 9-331 states that rights provided by Article 3 (negotiable instruments), Article 7 (documents of title), and Article 8 (investment proper-

---

1. *See,* § 9-327.
2. *See,* § 9-328 (including items such as securities and stocks).
3. *See,* § 9-329.
4. *See,* § 9-330 (including items such as negotiable drafts and notes).

ties) are not trumped by Article 9. Section 9-331(c) specifically states, "(c) [Filing not notice.] Filing under this article does not constitute notice of a claim or defense to the holders, or purchasers, or person described in [the above articles]." The following examples are based on Sections 9-318 to 9-322 and the associated comments and examples.

Example A

Generally a security interest only attaches to the rights that a granting debtor has. For example, a debtor may sell accounts or chattel paper to a buyer then sell the same to another party. If the first party fails to perfect and the second party does perfect, the second party prevails even though the selling seller had no interest at the time of the second sale. See, Section 9-318(b) and comment 6 to 9-203. However, if the secured party has a perfected floating security interest in the debtor's inventory and the debtor grants a security interest to a factor of accounts (intangibles), which is a type of filing collateral, the inventory financer's security interest attaches because the accounts are proceeds of inventory and automatically perfected if the security interest on the original collateral is perfected (§9-315).

The last described transaction may be diagramed as follows:

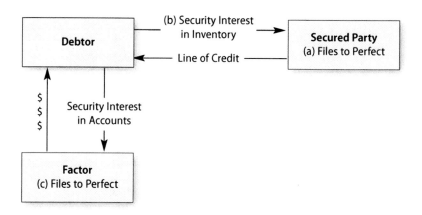

Questions

Problem 4.57

➤ Review the sequence of events. Why would the secured party have filed to perfect before it entered into a security agreement and gave value to Debtor?

Problem 4.58

➤ Who has priority to the accounts receivables, the Factor or the secured party?

➤ What might you need to know before you give a definite answer?

Problem 4.59

➤ Generally, why wouldn't a party secured by inventory have any objections to its debtor factoring accounts receivable?

Example B

If a secured party perfects its security interest in property such as investment property by filing and a competing secured party perfects by taking control, the competing secured party will prevail as to the collateral and any cash proceeds such as from sale or dividends placed in the debtor's deposit account (unless a bank pursuant to agreement or in exercise of its setoff right has taken control of the deposit account). If the first to file or perfect rule of §9-322(a)(1) were applied, the first secured party's security interest in the cash proceeds would be senior. If the first secured party had control of the debtor's deposit account (lock box situation), then the first secured party would have priority. Why? See, §9-327(1) and §9-315(d). For any non-filing collateral used as original collateral a secured party in possession or control will prevail over a secured party who files even if filing is a permitted perfection method. See, comments 7 and 8 to §9-322.

Example C

Lender has a perfected security interest in the equipment of a manufacturer. While upgrading, the manufacturer sells the equipment to a used equipment Dealer who subsequently sells to a BIOC. A BIOC takes free of a security interest created by his seller, here the used equipment dealer. But "his seller" did not create the security interest. The manufacturer did. And the manufacturer is not a merchant for the sale of his equipment. However, if the Lender learns of the sale to Dealer and does nothing, arguably the Lender has acquiesced. The BIOC might be able to rely on §2-403(2), "entrusting" in order to take free of the Lender's interest. The Lender, if he can trace the proceeds of the sale, is entitled to those proceeds. See, §§9-320(a) and 9-322(c).

Example D

Assume a secured party perfects its security interest by taking control of a deposit account. A second secured party thereafter advances money against the debtor's equipment and perfects by filing. Even if debtor used funds traceable to the deposit account to purchase the equipment, the second secured party wins because the party secured by the deposit account did not file as to equipment as original collateral. The first secured party will claim that the equipment was bought with his collateral (cash), hence, the equipment qualifies as proceeds of collateral but how would the equipment financer know that? A creditor making advances against equipment would do so after searching the U.C.C. records. He would not expect equipment to be claimed merely as proceeds without filing. Note that the PMSI financer (not in this example) may rely on the protections afforded by §9-324(b). Whenever, any problem arises with respect to claims to proceeds, the first step is to ascertain the classification of the collateral. Whether the original collateral was equipment or inventory may determine the outcome as between competing claimants.

Example E

Lender perfects a security interest in Debtor's inventory by filing a financing statement covering "inventory." Debtor sells the inventory and deposits the buyer's check into a deposit account. Debtor draws a check on the deposit account and uses it to pay for equipment. Under the "lowest intermediate balance rule," which is a permitted method of tracing in the relevant jurisdiction, see Comment 3 to §9-315, the funds used to pay for the equipment were identifiable proceeds of the inventory. Because the proceeds (equipment) were acquired with cash proceeds (deposit account), §9-315(d)(1) does not extend perfection beyond the 20-day automatic period.

Example F

Lender perfects a security interest in Debtor's inventory by filing a financing statement covering "all debtor's property." As in *Example E*, Debtor sells the inventory, deposits the buyer's check into a deposit account, draws a check on the deposit account, and uses the check to pay for equipment. Under the "lowest intermediate balance rule," which is a permitted method of tracing in the relevant jurisdiction, see, §9-315, comment 3, the funds used to pay for the equipment were identifiable proceeds of the inventory. Because the proceeds (equipment) were acquired with cash proceeds (deposit account), §9-315(d)(1) does not extend perfection beyond the 20-day automatic period. However, because the financing statement is sufficient to perfect a security interest in debtor's equipment, under §9-315(d)(3) the security interest in the equipment proceeds remains perfected beyond the 20-day period.

Do not confuse this 20 day rule with the 20 rule set forth in §9-312(e) and (f). *See*, Comment 7 to §9-312. That Comment makes clear that if goods are covered by a negotiable document Article 7 is applicable. The person who qualifies as a holder will prevail. *See*, §§1-201(20) and 7-102(9). The exception in §9-312(f) is for the convenience of a financing party after a bank or other financer gives up temporary possession in order for the goods to be sold and for its debtor to pay the financing party.

F. Simple Secured Financing

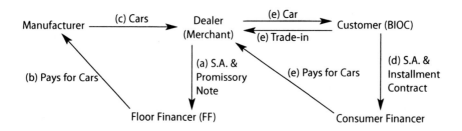

The letters below correspond to the letters in the diagram above. They describe the sequence of events in the simple secured financing hypothetical.

(a) This allows the Floor Financer to perfect the security interest, which is granted by debtor (the car dealer) in inventory. Floor Financer will not pay manufacturer until filing is checked.

(b) Once the Manufacturer is paid, it sends cars to the Dealer. At the point the Dealer (the Debtor of the Floor Financer) has rights in the collateral. The secured party (the Floor Financer) has given value and a security agreement granting a security interest was executed, hence the security interest of Floor Financer attaches. *See*, §9-203.

(c) Possession of cars change between parties to the transaction.

(d) Customer arranges financing through Consumer Financer, such as, Ally, Toyota Motor Credit, Customer's Bank, or a Credit Union, which then perfects.

(e) Customer arranges payment which includes sums from Consumer Financer and a trade in, together the proceeds of a sale. *See*, §9-102(a)(64). At that point the security interest of the Floor Financer is released in the car sold (here the consumer) who qualifies as a BIOC. Floor Financer's security interest then attaches to the proceeds, that is, cash plus trade in.

Questions

Problem 4.60

➤ Does Floor Financer's security interest follow the car bought by the BIOC?

➤ Does it attach to the proceeds?

➤ What are the proceeds?

Problem 4.61

➤ Is the Dealer a BIOC from the Manufacturer?

➤ How is the manufacturer classified: merchant, non-merchant businessman, or consumer?

Problem 4.62

➤ How does Floor Financer perfect its security interest in the Dealer's inventory?

Problem 4.63

➤ How does the Consumer Financer perfect its interest in the Customer's car?

Problem 4.64

➤ If the promissory note issued to the Floor Financer by the Dealer was used as collateral, how would a financing party perfect its interest?

Problem 4.65

➤ If the Consumer Financer sold all the installment contracts generated from its financing operation in order to raise more cash for loan purposes, how would the buyer of such installment contracts perfect its interest?

Problem 4.66

➤ In the scenario described in problem 4.62, who gets the right to repossess if the customer defaults on the installment contract?

G. Perfection Recap

Crucial to an understanding of the perfection rules is to understand that collateral is either tangible, quasi-tangible, sometimes referred to as quasi-intangible, or intangible. Then a determination of whether the collateral is fil-ing, non-filing collateral, or collateral that may be perfected in more than one way. For example, if filing collateral, can perfection be achieved other than by filing such as by possession? If so, does the method of perfection affect the pri-ority of security interests? What are the exceptions to first in time, first in right? And does it make a difference if the collateral is original collateral or proceeds of collateral?

Section 9-201 governs the rights of secured creditors as against others in a general way. Subsections 9-201 (b) and (c) subject the Article 9 rules to cer-tain non-U.C.C. law, most specifically, consumer protection laws that are in-consistent with Article 9. Section 9-204 governs with respect to after-acquired property and future advances. It specifically protects consumers from an after-acquired property clause except for goods received by a consumer within ten days of a secured party giving value or for an accession.

Questions

Problem 4.67

➤ Under what circumstances would a secured creditor want its security interest to "float" over after-acquired property?

➤ Is it necessary to explicitly provide for an after-acquired property clause? Give authority for your answer.

Problem 4.68

➤ What is an accession?

➤ Distinguish an accession from commingled goods. *See,* §§9-335, 9-336.

➤ Give an example of each.

Several Georgia Code Sections follow:

O.C.G.A. §44-14-363. *Special liens on personalty; notice; enforcement; priorities; maximum claims for storage; recordation.*

(a) All mechanics of every sort shall have a special lien on personal property for work done and material furnished in manufacturing or repairing the personal property and for storage of the personal prop-erty after its manufacture or repair, which storage begins accruing after 30 days' written notice to the owner of the fact that storage is accruing and of the daily dollar amount thereof; and said notice shall be mailed to the owner by certified mail or statutory overnight de-livery addressed to the owner at his last known address. Such special liens may be asserted by the retention of the personal property or the mechanic may surrender the personal property and give credit when the lien is enforced in accordance with Code Section 44-14-550; and if such special liens are asserted by retention of the personal property, the mechanic shall not be required to surrender the property to the holder of a subordinate security interest or lien. Such liens shall be superior to all liens except liens for taxes and, except as provided in subsection (2) of Code Section 11-9-310, such other liens as the mechanic may have had actual notice of before the work was done or material furnished.

(b) The maximum amount of storage that may be charged shall be $1.00 per day. Nothing contained in this Code section shall allow a fee for storage to be charged on any item with a fair market value in excess of $200.00. Storage charges pursuant to this Code section shall not apply to motor vehicles now or hereafter covered by Chapter 3 of Title 40 nor shall the storage fee be charged if there is a bona fide dispute between the customer and the mechanic as to the manner of repair or the charges for repair.

(c)(1) When possession of the property is surrendered to the debtor, the mechanic shall record his or her claim of lien within 90 days after the work is done and the material is furnished or, in the case of repairs made on or to farm machinery, within 180 days after the work is done and the material is furnished. The claim of lien shall be recorded in the office of the clerk of the superior court of the county where the owner of the property resides. The claim shall be in substance as follows:

"A.B., mechanic, claims a lien on (here describe the property) of C.B., for work done, material furnished, and storage accruing (as the case may be) in manufacturing, repairing, and storing (as the case may be) the same."

(2) If possession of the personal property subject to a special lien as provided in this Code section is surrendered to the debtor and if such special lien is not preserved by recording the claim of lien as provided in paragraph (1) of this subsection, the mechanic acquires a special lien on other personal property belonging to the debtor which comes into the possession of the mechanic, except that this sentence shall not apply to consumer goods which are being used by a consumer for personal, family, or household purposes or which have been bought by a consumer for use for personal, family, or household purposes. The special lien created by this paragraph shall be subject to the provisions of this Code section as to foreclosure and recording.

O.C.G.A. § 11-9-310. *When filing required to perfect security interest or agricultural lien; security interests and agricultural liens to which filing provisions do not apply.*

> (a) *General rule; perfection by filing.* Except as otherwise provided in subsection (b) of this Code section and subsection (b) of Code Section 11-9-312, a financing statement must be filed to perfect all security interests and agricultural liens.

> (b) *Exceptions; filing not necessary.* The filing of a financing statement is not necessary to perfect a security interest:

> (1) That is perfected under subsection (d), (e), (f), or (g) of Code Section 11-9-308;

> (2) That is perfected under Code Section 11-9-309 when it attaches; ...

See, O.C.G.A. § 11-9-309. *Security interest perfected upon attachment.*

O.C.G.A. § 11-9-333(b) *Mechanics' liens on farm machinery.*

> A mechanics' lien on farm machinery or equipment arising on or after July 1, 1985, shall have priority over any perfected security interest in such farm machinery or equipment unless a financing statement has been filed as provided in Code Section 11-9-501 and unless the financing statement describes the particular piece of farm machinery or equipment to which the perfected security interest applies. Such description may include the make, model, and serial number of the piece of farm machinery or equipment. However, such description shall be sufficient whether or not it is specific if it reasonably identifies what is described and a mistake in such description shall not invalidate the description if it provides a key to identifying the farm machinery or equipment.

Question

Problem 4.69

> ➤ Applying the previous Georgia Code sections, who has priority? Is it the Finance Company that has a perfected Security interest in your car or the mechanic who has possession of your car because you failed to pay for the new tires he installed? Explain.

Discussion

Section 9-317 deals with competing priorities between and among secured creditors, lien creditors, and agricultural lien holders. Section 9-322 governs the priority rights of secured creditors and should be read with §§ 9-324 and 9-317 on the promotion of properly perfected purchase money secured creditors. Section 9-320 provides protection from secured creditors for a BIOC or as a result of a casual or consumer-to-consumer sale except if § 9-320(b)(4) applies. Note, however, § 9-320(e), "Possessory Security Interest not Affected" if § 9-313 applies covering quasi-tangibles, tangible chattel paper, money, and certificated securities.

Generally, first to file or perfect in anyway is first in priority except as otherwise provided in § 9-322. Perfection as to the collateral, such as, inventory or equipment, perfects as to proceeds generated from the sale of collateral.

Questions

Problem 4.70

➤ If a party secured by inventory establishes a revolving line of credit or otherwise gives the debtor/obligor future advances, does that secured party have to file a new financing statement? Give authority for your answer.

➤ Does the secured party have to execute a new security agreement?

➤ Does the secured party have to provide for a new or modified monetary obligation?

Example and Questions

Debtor commences negotiations with the Bank on August 1, 2009. A security agreement for a $500,000 capital loan collateralized by "all equipment now held or hereinafter acquired" is executed and the funds are advanced on August 24, 2009 at which time the Bank files a financing statement with an adequate description of the collateral.

The Debtor, believing that the Bank will not loan the money begins negotiations with Capital Finance Company on August 16, 2009, whereupon Capital Finance Company files a financing statement covering "all equipment now held or hereinafter acquired." A security agreement is executed on August 25, 2009 and $200,000 is advanced to the Debtor.

TIME LINE

• August 1, 2009   Debtor negotiates with Bank of America

• August 16, 2009   Debtor negotiates with Capital Finance
                        Company

- August 16, 2009   Capital Finance Company files UCC #1
- August 24, 2009   Bank of America files UCC #1
- August 24, 2009   Bank of America advances funds pursuant to agreement
- August 25, 2009   Capital Finance Company advances funds pursuant to agreement

Questions

Problem 4.71

➤ Whose security interest attached first?

Problem 4.72

➤ Whose perfection is effective at the earlier date, Bank's or Capital Finance Company's? Explain.

Discussion

The security interest follows the collateral except if otherwise provided by law. An exception occurs when a BIOC buys from a Seller in the Ordinary Course. The buyer buys free of the security interest created by the seller merchant in favor of the merchant's Finance Company, usually called the Floor Financer. *See,* §9-320.

A financing statement may be amended pursuant to §9-512(a). The Official Code of Georgia applies Alternative A. If the amendment adds a debtor or collateral priority will date from the filing of the amendment as to that new debtor or new collateral.

Termination statements must be filed pursuant to §9-513 once the debtor's/obligor's obligations are met. Note that there are separate rules for parties secured by consumer goods versus parties secured by other personal property. If a secured party fails to comply with Article 9, §9-625 sets forth recoverable damages.

A financing statement not otherwise misleading that becomes misleading after filing, such as a debtor's changed use of collateral from a consumer good to equipment, is not rendered ineffective. *See,* §§9-506 and 9-507.

If the debtor's name is changed or a new debtor succeeds the original debtor, the secured party has four months to amend a seriously misleading F.S. in order for his security interest to continue in collateral, such as a floating lien over inventory acquired by the debtor after the four-month period. A new debtor might be created because of a change in structure, for example, from a sole proprietorship to a LP or LLC, or after a merger. This four-month rule does not apply if the original debtor transfers the collateral to a third party in violation of the security agreement or otherwise.

If the debtor's location changes, the four-month rule applies under § 9-316. If the debtor becomes a new debtor in another jurisdiction, for example a Georgia corporation reincorporates in Delaware, then the secured party has one year to file in the new jurisdiction.

Example and Questions

Debtor is a general partnership located in South Carolina. Lender properly perfects a security interest in equipment in South Carolina on May 15, 2002. Debtor moves to Georgia on April 2, 2005.

Questions

Problem 4.73

➤ How long does the Lender have to perfect in Georgia before such Lender becomes unperfected?

Problem 4.74

➤ What if the Debtor didn't move until April 2, 2007?

Debtor is a Georgia Corporation. Lender has a perfected security interest in all of the Debtor's equipment and inventory dating from May 15, 2002. On June 8, 2004, Debtor reincorporated in Delaware, dissolving the Georgia Corporation without a name change.

Problem 4.75

➤ How long does the Lender have to re-perfect? Must Lender re-perfect?

Problem 4.76

➤ If the Lender does re-perfect on March 16, 2004, on what date is its perfection effective?

Problem 4.77

➤ What if the Lender re-perfects on May 17, 2003?

Problem 4.78

➤ If a Buyer buys some of Debtor's equipment on November 10, 2004, does it take free of or subject to the Lender's security interest?

Problem 4.79

➤ Under what circumstances could the Lender rely on §9-609?

H. Future Advances—§9-323

This section deals with security agreements that provide for future advances which are made after a third party acquires an interest in the collateral, such as, a judgment lien creditor or the IRS with a tax lien. The first to file rule of §9-322(a)(i) relates any future advances back to the initial perfection, hence, as a general rule an intervening secured party or lien creditor does not prime a previously perfected party giving future advances with the exception of perfected PMSI financers following the appropriate procedures and those financers of non-filing collateral as set-forth previously. Under §9-323(a), assuming perfection of the initial secured party, the time of the advance may not relate back if the perfection relied upon was automatic under §9-309 or temporary under §9-312(e), (f), or (g) (temporary relinquishment of possession of non-filing collateral or of goods perfected by possession for the purpose related to sale) unless the advance is made pursuant to commitment.

A lien creditor including the trustee in a bankruptcy will prime a previously perfected secured party "to the extent that the security interest secures an advance made more than 45 days after the person becomes a lien creditor unless the advance is made without knowledge of the lien or it is made pursuant to a commitment without knowledge of the lien." §9-323(b) Compare this with the rules applicable to commercial financing security under the federal tax lien where new collateral (not cash) comes into the possession of a debtor after the 45th day after tax lien filing. In this instance, the new collateral "feeds" the tax lien. The above rules do not apply to buyers of accounts, chattel paper, payment intangibles, promissory notes or to a consignor of goods. Why so? A chattel paper financer usually doesn't check the U.C.C. or lien records. Promissory notes are freely negotiated (negotiable instruments) or otherwise transferred. A sale of accounts generates cash, which is exactly what the competing creditors want.

Under a proper reading of the first to file or perfect rule of §9-322(a)(1), it is clear that the time when an advance is made plays no role in determining priorities among conflicting security interests except when a financing statement was not filed. Thus, a secured party takes subject to all advances secured by a competing security interest having priority under §9-322(a)(1). This result generally obtains regardless of how the competing security interest is perfected and regardless of whether the advances are made pursuant to commitment. *See,* §9-102.

Case Example and Questions

On February 1st, Secured Party (1) makes an advance secured by machinery in the Debtor's possession and files a financing statement. On March 1st, Secured Party (2) makes an advance secured by the same machinery and files a financing statement. On April 1st, Secured Party (1) makes an additional advance, under the original security agreement, against the same machinery. Secured Party (1) has priority pursuant to the first to file or perfect rule of §9-322(a)(1), since he was the first to file. Secured Party (1)'s security interest has priority over Secured Party (2)'s February 1st and April 1st advance. It makes no difference whether Secured Party (1) knows of Secured Party (2)'s intervening advance when Secured Party (1) is the first to file or perfect.

The following is based on *AEG Liquidation Trust v. Toobro N.Y. LLC et al.,* 932 N.Y.S.2d 759 (Sup. Ct. 2011).

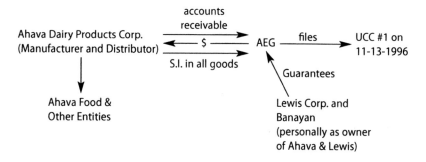

Order of Events and Questions

Problem 4.80

➤ On November 6, 1996, AEG and Ahava Dairy entered into a factoring agreement. What is a factoring agreement?

➤ What is the difference between a sale and an assignment of account receivables, that is, between recourse and non-recourse factoring?

Problem 4.81

➤ Personal guarantees in favor of AEG were signed by Lewis Corp. and Banayan (personally as owner of Ahava and Lewis Corp.). What is a personal guarantee? Is there any collateral used in these transactions?

Problem 4.82

➤ On November 21, 2000, AEG filed a Chapter 11 Bankruptcy petition. Ahava Dairy owed $8 million plus under the factoring agreement.

Problem 4.83

➤ On April 17, 2001, AEG, as Debtor in possession, filed a complaint against Ahava Dairy, Lewis and Banayan, and later amended it to include Ahava Food. What is a debtor in possession?

Problem 4.84

➤ On February 7, 2002, termination statements (UCC #2) purporting to terminate AEG's security interest were filed, apparently by Ahava Dairy and Lewis Corp. What is the effect of a termination statement?

Problem 4.85

➤ Meanwhile from 2000 onward, Banayan and his brother created other entities, including Ahava of California, which were transferees of various assets from Ahava Dairy and Banayan. Does Bankruptcy Code §544(b) or 548 apply to these transactions? Explain.

Further, according to AEG's complaint, "in 2003, whilst in the midst of active litigation with AEG…, Banayan formed St. Lawrence." According to the complaint, St. Lawrence was an alter ego of the three original Ahava entities — Ahava Dairy, Ahava Food, and Lewis — having the same ownership and management structure as these entities and marketing the same products to the same customers. Plaintiff alleges that, through the course of the years, St. Lawrence received assets of the three original Ahava entities — Ahava Dairy, Ahava Food, and Lewis. The transfer of assets and the creation of new entities continued through 2007. In 2005, Signature Bank became a creditor of the various transferees and filed UCC #1s. On July 28, 2006, AEG filed Correction Statements pursuant to §9-518 stating that the termination statements were unauthorized.

AEG Liquidation Trust v. Toobro N.Y. LLC

WL 2535035 (N.Y. Sup. 2011)

(edited and citations omitted)

KORNREICH, J.

On June 18, 2008, Signature Bank sent a "Notice of Secured Party Sale" (Notice of Sale) to a list of entities pursuant to U.C.C. 9-613. The Notice of Sale indicated that "the collateral described below on Schedule A … will be sold at a sale … held to enforce the rights of Lender as Secured Party Seller in the Collateral." The Notice of Sale further stated that the "Collateral is the subject of a certain Security Agreement dated as of August 5, 2005, by and among Ahava

Food, St. Lawrence, Lewis, and Schwartz (collectively the Debtor') and the Lender."

Schedule A indicated that "Collateral" meant:

> *all personal property and fixtures* of *each Debtor in which the Debtor has an interest,* in each case whether now or hereafter existing or now owned or hereafter acquired and whether subject to the Uniform Commercial Code including all goods, money, instruments, accounts, farm products, inventory, equipment, documents, chattel paper, securities and general intangibles and all interest, dividends and other distributions thereon paid and payable in cash or in property; and all replacements and substitutions for, and all accessions and additions to, and all products and Proceeds of, all the foregoing. [emphasis supplied]

* * *

On June 25, 2008, AEG's counsel sent a letter to [Signature Bank's Counsel] advising it that AEG was a secured creditor of Ahava Dairy and Lewis pursuant to a 1996 security agreement and UCC [#]1 financing statements filed on November 13, 1996. [AEG] further advised that AEG is a judgment creditor of Ahava Dairy, Lewis and related entities pursuant to a judgment dated March 10, 2008. Finally, Dickstein's letter advised [Signature Bank] that AEG claimed priority over the purported lien of Signature Bank and that any action taken by Herrick [Signature Bank's Counsel], Signature Bank, or its agents that "would infringe upon or purport to affect, negate or modify AEG's interest in the subject collateral would constitute a breach of the automatic stay of Section 362 of the Bankruptcy Code."

* * *

[The Court then discussed various theories of liability based upon *alter ego,* the guarantees, successor liability and *de facto* merger. For purposes of this course, only the Article 9 issues will be addressed.]

[The collateral at issue was sold and the proceeds were placed in the registry of the court. The proceeds were not sufficient to eliminate AEG's debt.] Section 9-315 of the Uniform Commercial Code (U.C.C.) provides that "a security interest ... continues in collateral notwithstanding sale ... or other disposition thereof ... *and* a security interest attaches to any identifiable proceeds of collateral." [emphasis supplied] *See,* U.C.C. §9-315(a)(1)-(2). Exceptions to this rule exist where the secured party authorized the sale free of the security interests or the buyer purchased the goods in the ordinary course of business. *See,* U.C.C. §§9-315(a)(1), 2-403(2). Neither exception applies here. Consequently, defendants cannot infer that the security interests did not continue in the collateral. The Bankruptcy Court Order merely reflected the statutory requirement that upon sale of the collateral, the security interests *also* attach to the proceeds. *See,* U.C.C. §9-315(a)(2). It does not address the status of the security interests in the underlying collateral and could not eliminate the statutory protection of Section 9-315.

Defendants next argue that AEG's security interests in the assets of Ahava Dairy and Lewis were "discharged" as a result of the July 9, 2008 secured party sale of these assets by Signature Bank. This argument is also unavailing. Section 9-617 of the U.C.C. provides that "a secured party's disposition of collateral after default ... discharges any *subordinate* security interest or other subordinate lien." [emphasis supplied] *See,* U.C.C. §9-617(a)(3). Defendants fail to show that AEG's security interests in Ahava Dairy's and/or Lewis' assets were subordinate to those of Signature Bank.

To explain, U.C.C. 9-317(a)(1) provides that "a security interest ... is subordinate to the rights of: (1) a person entitled to priority under Section 9-322...." Section 9-322(a)(1) provides that "priority among conflicting security interests ... in the same collateral is determined according to the following rules: (1) Conflicting perfected security interests ... *rank according to priority in time of filing or perfection...*" [emphasis supplied]. AEG perfected the security interests by filing UCC-1 financing statements on November 13, 1996. Signature Bank perfected its security interests by filing UCC-1 financing statements in 2005. Hence, defendants fail to show that AEG's security interests are subordinate to those of Signature Bank under U.C.C. §9-317. *See,* U.C.C. §§9-317(a)(1), 9-322(a)(1). *A fortiori,* they fail to show that Signature Bank's disposition of these assets through the secured party sale of July 9, 2008 discharged AEG's security interests in the collateral. *See,* U.C.C. §9-617(a)(3).

The filing of the UCC-3 termination statements on February 7, 2002 does not change this result. Section 9-513(d) of the U.C.C. provides that "[e]xcept as otherwise provided in Section 9-510, upon the filing of a termination statement with the filing office, the financing statement to which the termination statement relates ceases to be effective." Section 9-510(a), however, provides that "[a] filed record is effective only to the extent that it was filed by a person that may file it under Section 9-509." Under Section 9-509(d)(1) & (2),

A person may file an amendment other than an amendment that adds collateral covered by a financing statement or an amendment that adds a debtor to the financing statement only if:

(1) the *secured party of record authorizes the filing;* or

(2) the amendment is a termination statement for a financing statement as to which *the secured party of record has failed to file or send a termination statement as required by section 9-513(a) or*

(c), the debtor authorizes the filing, and the termination statement indicates that the debtor authorized it to be filed. [emphasis supplied]

Neither condition for "effectiveness" of the termination statements is met here.

AEG as the secured party did not authorize the filing of the termination statements. *See,* U.C.C. §9-509(d)(1). Nor did AEG fail to file or send a termination statement under U.C.C. §9-509(d)(2) because Sections 9-513(a) and (c) do not apply in this case. Section 9-513(a) does not apply because that section applies to consumer goods. The underlying collateral here was not consumer goods. Section 9-513(c), in turn, requires

20 days after a secured party receives an authenticated demand from a debtor, the secured party shall cause the secured party of record for a financing statement to send to the debtor a termination statement for the financing statement or file the termination statement *if:* (1) ... *there is no obligation secured by the collateral covered by the financing statement....* [Emphasis supplied.]

* * *

Questions

Problem 4.86

➤ The security interest of AEG was perfected on November 13, 1996. What prevented the UCC #1 filing from automatically terminating by November 12, 2001? *See,* 9-510(c).

Problem 4.87

➤ If a settlement agreement had been entered by order of the court reducing the amount owed from $8 million plus to $5 million payable over time, may AEG still claim the entire $8 million?

➤ What does this depend upon? Explain.

Problem 4.88

➤ How could Signature Bank have protected itself?

Problem 4.89

➤ How did AEG perfect its security interests in Ahava Dairy's accounts receivable? How did it perfect as to all the other assets?

Problem 4.90

➤ Explain in your own words how §§9-317(a)(1) and 9-322(a)(1) compare.

Problem 4.91

➤ Assets were transferred by Ahava Dairy to a number of different entities, which may have had secured creditors including Signature Bank. Why didn't the four month or one year rule of § 9-316 apply?

I. Inventory Financing

1. Introduction

The following diagram details a basic inventory financing transaction. This diagram and type of transaction will be used in the subsequent material.

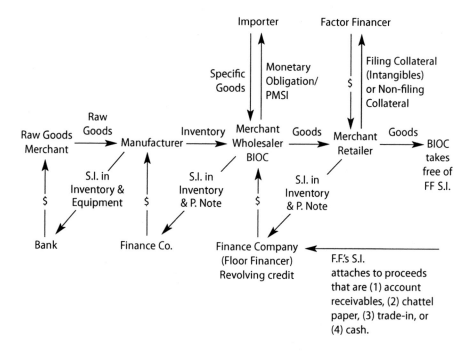

2. Tax Liens

Secured Parties with filing collateral check for liens filed against their Debtor every 45 days. A Federal Tax lien is the most serious problem and Judicial Liens are also a matter of concern. Inventory arriving after the 45th day "feeds" the tax lien. As to a judgment lien, see §9-323(b) dealing with future advances made 45 days after a person becomes a lien creditor as defined in §9-102(52).

3. Financing

If an Importer properly perfects his PMSI in inventory, his interest in that part of the inventory he supplied will prime the security interest of the Floor Financier. In order to properly perfect, the Importer must complete two tasks including: (1) give notice to the Floor Financier that a PMSI is created as to the specific goods; and (2) file the UCC #1 prior to the Wholesaler or other selling merchant receiving the specific goods.

A Finance Company is likely to sell off its chattel paper and notes if the Merchant Retailer does not. If the note is negotiable it can be bundled with similar securities and monetary obligations, which can then be securitized.

Merchant Retailer and Merchant Wholesaler might also have an Equipment Financer, usually a bank, which may have a PMSI in specific pieces of equipment. If the bank or finance company lends money against already existing equipment or provides for the security interest to attach to subsequently acquired equipment whether or not such secured party is obligated for future advances, a PMSI is not created In any case the Debtor (Retailer or Wholesaler) will grant the bank a security interest by signing a security agreement and a promissory note setting forth the monetary obligation.

A lender secured by equipment, rather than inventory does not automatically release its interest upon sale of the equipment by its debtor. The item of equipment sold is not free of the secured party's interest. If the security interest is in inventory, then the merchant or Seller in the Ordinary Course who created the interest sells the item free of that interest to a BIOC. In any case, the security interest automatically attaches to proceeds.

Chattel paper can be sold free of the floor financier's interest as long as the purchaser (buyer or assignee) gives value and takes possession unless the chattel paper, on its face, says it is non-assignable.

4. Factor Financing: The Sale or Assignment of Receivables

Factoring: Sale of Receivables

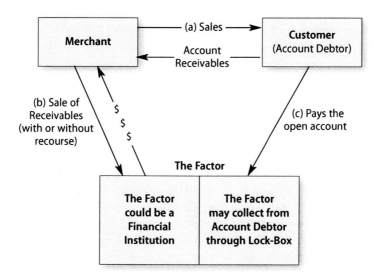

If a receivable is sold with **recourse**, the Factor may "sell" the receivable of a defaulting customer back to the merchant. Recourse receivables financing are often referred to as an assignment to a Factor rather than a sale.

A lock-box is a Post Office box that is accessible by the bank. A company may set up a lock box service with their bank for receiving customer payments. The company's customers send their payments to the PO Box. Then the bank collects and processes these payments directly depositing them to the company's account. Such accounts, although in the Debtor's name, may be controlled by a Factor, with proceeds in excess of what is owed to the Factor then deposited in the Debtor's operating account.

5. Collateralized Borrowing

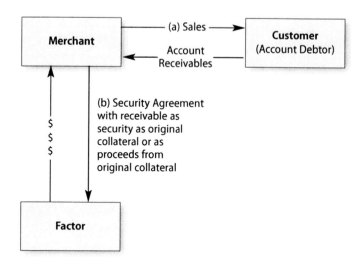

Merchant will be obligated to pay back the loan pursuant to the agreed terms. Similar to the previous diagramed example, if the receivables are proceeds of the original collateral, and a party secured by inventory is perfected, the Factor must get the secured party's permission to prime the inventory secured party's interest.

Questions

Problem 4.92

➤ In which example above has the merchant surrendered control over collecting on the receivables?

Problem 4.93

➤ Why might a factor or a financial institution factoring receivables insist on a lock-box? *Hint: Isn't the lock-box analogous to a deposit account if the secured party keeps control?*

6. Protecting the Proceeds: Review

When does the Floor Financier lose perfection in proceeds? Note, again, that §9-315(c) provides that a security interest perfected in the original collateral perfects the interest in proceeds. This perfection continues unless the proceeds are not cash proceeds, not directly exchanged for the collateral, or not of the same type as the original collateral. If cash proceeds are no longer identifiable, that is, no accounting method could trace them, or the cash is spent in the ordinary course of business, or a bank sets-off against the cash pursuant to its statutory right of set-off, then the Floor Financer loses. A Floor Financer will also lose if a deposit account is controlled by someone other than the debtor or Floor Financer. If a debtor spends cash proceeds on items other than inventory, that is, the collateral subject to its security interest, the Floor Financer must re-perfect against that different type of collateral (say a piece of equipment) within 20 days. See, §9-315(d). If, however, a debtor exchanges covered collateral for other than cash, the secured party's interest continues since anything exchanged for collateral are proceeds.

When commingled proceeds (usually cash) are identifiable, they may be reachable if traced. Perfection as to the original collateral will perfect as to proceeds of any kind directly exchanged and the proceeds even if they are proceeds of proceeds (example: cash proceeds are exchanged for inventory) of the same type as the original collateral. See, §9-322(c).

If the proceeds of proceeds are of a type not covered by the original filing, then the secured party has 20 days to perfect and maintain its priority.

Cash proceeds from the sale of inventory are subject to the Floor Financer prior perfected security interest even if a tax lien is filed and the 45 day period of protection is over. However, if new inventory is purchased on the 46th day after tax lien filing, even if it is of the same type as the original collateral, the IRS will prevail as to that inventory—it "feeds" the tax lien. See, 26 U.S.C. §6323.

J. Fixtures and Article 9 of the U.C.C., §9-334

1. Fixture Filing

Fixtures are defined in §9-102(a)(41) as "goods that have become so related to particular real property that an interest in them arises under real property law." Put another way, fixtures are those items of personal property that become so related to the real estate that title to such items would pass with a deed to the real estate. A security interest in fixtures or goods that are to become fixtures may be created under Article 9 with perfection at the debtor's location or through a fixture filing in the jurisdiction where the land is located. A fixture filing must be made in the landowner's name.

2. Real Estate

General Rule: § 9-334(c). The owner or buyer of real estate defeats a secured creditor with a security interest perfected under Article 9.

General Rule: § 9-334(h). A construction money mortgage holder, that is, the entity financing the construction and any refinancer, takes priority over any party secured by a fixture after the construction mortgage is filed and before completion of the construction regardless of whether perfection is under Article 9 or by a fixture filing.

Why? In both cases the buyer or financer of construction expects to have an interest in the real estate that is not encumbered.

3. PMSI and Fixtures

For information regarding PMSIs, see § 9-334(d). This section is about the replacement of an original fixture or previous fixture by a debtor in possession of the real property or if the debtor has an interest of record in the real property. The usual PMSI rules apply, however, if the owner voluntarily transfers the real property to another and the creditor has not perfected by a fixture filing as opposed to an Article 9 filing, the new transferee (owner) will prevail. See § 9-334(e)(1). For example, assume Bank finances a heating system that replaces the existing heating system in a building. Bank does a fixture filing. A subsequent purchaser (encumbrancer or buyer) would take subject to the Bank's interest.

Why? The subsequent purchaser would have notice of the new heating system by a search of the real estate records. That purchaser would know it is not original construction but rather new, enhancing the value of the building. Insofar as money was still owed, the new purchaser would negotiate a price reduction or require the Bank to be paid off from sale proceeds.

4. Trade Fixtures and Consumer Goods

Section 9-334(e)(2) dealing with trade fixtures and consumer goods provides that certain perfected security interests will have priority over an encumbrancer or owner of real property if:

before the goods become fixtures, the security interest is perfected by any method permitted by this article and the fixtures are readily removable:

(a) factory or office machines;

(b) equipment that is not primarily used or leased for use in the operation of real property; or

(c) replacements of domestic appliances that are consumer goods.

Perfection is under Article 9, and perfection must occur before any of the goods are converted into fixtures, such as a replacement appliance that is built in. In that case, a fixture filing might be necessary even though the statute says "perfection is by any method." However, under real estate law the mortgage deed will grant the lender an interest in the real property "together with the tenements, hereditaments, and appurtenances, thereunto belonging, or in anywise appertaining," which any covers fixtures including those after-acquired.

As a practical matter even if the holder of a perfected security interest in goods that become fixtures has priority (claiming a PMSI), that secured creditor has these options:

1. Remove and repair the real property. *See*, § 9-604(c); or

2. Claim the sale price was increased by the value of its fixture and claim a share of the proceeds measured by the lesser of the value added or the debt owed from the seller. *See*, § 9-604(b)(2).

5. Lien Creditors and Trustees in Bankruptcy

The rights of lien creditors and the bankruptcy trustee are set forth in § 9-334(e)(3). The applicable rule is first in time first in right. Either would lose to a properly perfected interest, regardless of how perfected, if perfected before the lien or interest of the trustee arises unless the act of perfection itself runs afoul of another Bankruptcy Code section.

K. Federal Tax Lien Statute
26 U.S.C. §§ 6321–6323

1. General

Federal law determines whether the lien attaches and its priority. State law determines whether property belongs to the taxpayer. Federal law "attaches consequences, federally defined, to rights created under state law." *Aquilino v. U.S.*, 363 U.S. 509 (1960). The lien arises after demand and attaches to all property, but the lien actually arises on assessment, hence is, in effect, a secret lien. *See*, 26 U.S.C. §§ 6321, 6322.

2. Priority

First in time first in right applies. Priority actually dates from filing by the IRS as if the lien were a mortgage on real property or a security interest in personality. See, 26 U.S.C. §6323(f). Even if the lien is filed, it is subordinate (the Internal Revenue Code states "not ... valid") to certain other liens, certain security interests, and purchasers including but not limited to:

a.   Purchasers of securities;

b.   Purchasers of motor vehicles in the purchaser's possession without notice of the tax lien;

c.   Personal property purchased at retail in good faith;

d.   Personal property purchased in a casual sale;

e.   Personal property subject to a possessory lien;

f.   Statutory real estate taxes if local law promotes them over a mortgage prior in time; or

g.   Certain others. *See,* 26 U.S.C. §6323(b).

Note: Purchaser is defined essentially as a buyer under the U.C.C. or lessee of real property. Other lien holders or parties acquiring a security interest are not purchasers for tax lien purposes. *See,* 26 U.S.C. §6323(h)(6).

Secured parties under Article 9 of the U.C.C. and parties secured by real estate mortgages (those involved in "commercial transactions financing agreements."): If these parties are properly perfected under state law prior to tax lien filing, they continue to have priority over the tax lien for any collateral acquired by the debtor "before the 46th day after the date of tax lien filing." After that, any new collateral coming into possession of the debtor "feeds" the tax lien.

This 46th day rule does not apply to an "obligatory disbursement agreement," that is when the taxpayer subject to the tax lien is "required" to make disbursements "by reason of the intervention of the rights of a person other than the tax payer."

Note: You cannot understand the tax lien statute unless you understand that for tax lien purposes there can be no security interest in collateral until the debtor actually gets the collateral. In other words, if Floor Planner has a security interest in all new car inventory now held or hereinafter acquired by dealer, for tax lien purposes there is no security interest in those cars until the dealer actually gets the car. See, 26 U.S.C. §6323(h)(i) which defines security interest as:

(1) Security Interest. The term "security interest" means any interest in property acquired by contract for the purpose of securing payment

or performance of an obligation or indemnifying against loss or liability. A security interest exists at any time.

(a) If, at such time, the property is in existence and the interest has become protected under local law against a subsequent judgment lien arising out of an unsecured obligation, and

(b) to the extent that, at such time, the holder has parted with money or money's worth.

Note: It seems that inventory, contract rights, and accounts receivables are regarded as separate property by the Federal Tax Lien Act. *See,* 26 U.S.C. §6323(c)(3)(B)(ii).

On the other hand, as indicated above, the tax lien statute does recognize certain priorities established under the U.C.C. and other state statutes.

Chapter Five

Foreclosure and Disposition of Collateral

A. Introduction

The security agreement generally will contain a definition of what events constitute a default. These events include:

1. Payment default,
2. False or misleading representations by the debtor or obligator,
3. Covenant default, such as violating a promise not to incur additional debt,
4. Having tax or judgment lien filed against the debtor or obligator, or
5. Bankruptcy of the debtor or obligator.

The debtor and obligator is generally the same person. If certain property, such as leasehold interests or trademarks, is to be excluded from a blanket security interest, the security agreement should so provide.

In order to protect itself and to effectively act as a secured party may include the following in its security agreement:

Secured Party Appointed Attorney-In-Fact: The Grantor hereby appoints the Secured Party the Grantor's attorney-in-fact, with full authority in the place and stead of the Grantor and in the name of the Grantor or otherwise, from time to time [during the continuance of an Event of Default] in the Secured Party's discretion to take any action and to execute any instrument which the Secured Party may deem necessary or advisable to accomplish the purposes of this Agreement (but the Secured Party shall not be obligated to and shall have no liability to the Grantor or any third party for failure to do so or take action). This appointment, being coupled with an interest, shall be irrevocable. The Grantor hereby ratifies all that said attorneys shall lawfully do or cause to be done by virtue hereof.

In general a secured party's remedies may vary, depending upon the circumstance and the exercise of its rights under the above paragraph:

- Collection: the secured party directly collects payments from parties owing amounts to the grantor of the security interest under third-party contracts.
- Disposition: the secured party sells or disposes of collateral at a private or public sale and retains the proceeds.
- Retention: the secured party retains the collateral in satisfaction of the debt.

In re Dalebout

454 B.R. 158 (Bankr. D. Kan. 2011)
(edited; most footnotes omitted)

KARLIN, Bankruptcy Judge

On or about April 10, 2006, Debtor Jody Lynn Dalebout ("Dalebout") entered into a Charge Slip contract with Wells Fargo Financial National Bank ("Wells Fargo") for the financing of the purchase and installation of six windows from American Exteriors, LLC. Contemporaneously with the creation of this contract, Dalebout completed and signed a Home Projects Visa Credit Card Account Application ("credit application"). The signature paragraph on the credit application stated that "you give us and we will retain a purchase-money security interest in the goods purchased under this Agreement."

* * *

You agree that any property described in this charge slip will remain personal property and will not become a fixture even if attached to real property.

The terms for the Home Project Visa Credit Card contain general terms, including:

> *Security Interest:* To the extent permitted by applicable law, you hereby grant to us and we are retaining a money security interest under the Uniform Commercial Code in the merchandise purchased on your account.... If you do not make a minimum payment due on your account by the date on which it was due, we may repossess any merchandise that has not been paid in full.

Dalebout used the Home Projects Visa credit card from Wells Fargo to pay for the six windows.

The windows were installed at Debtor's residence at 2216 Lawrence Road, Manhattan, Kansas. Dalebout was the owner of the residence at all relevant times. The windows were installed as replacement windows for the windows originally installed in Dalebout's home.

Debtors filed their Chapter 13 bankruptcy petition on October 6, 2010. Debtors listed Wells Fargo as an unsecured creditor in their bankruptcy schedules. Debtors' Chapter 13 plan did not identify Wells Fargo as a secured creditor or provide for payment of Wells Fargo's claim as a secured claim. Wells Fargo has not filed an objection to that plan.

Wells Fargo filed an initial proof of claim, claiming it was owed a secured debt of $6,426.36. Debtors objected to this proof of claim on the basis that because the windows were installed in their home, they had become fixtures. Debtors contended that because Wells Fargo did not have a mortgage on their property, the debt secured by the fixtures to the real estate was unsecured.

Wells Fargo does not claim any security interest in Debtors' real property and readily admits that it did not seek to protect its interest in the windows through either a fixture filing or a mortgage on Debtors' homestead. Instead, Wells Fargo contends that it maintains its security interest in the windows as consumer goods under the Kansas Uniform Commercial Code, §84-9-102(a)(23), and that it perfected its interest upon attachment under §84-9-309(1).

* * *

CONCLUSIONS OF LAW

The issue before the Court is whether Wells Fargo has a security interest in the windows Dalebout purchased using the Home Projects Visa credit card issued by Wells Fargo. The main question in resolving that issue is whether the windows are the personal property of Debtors, or whether they have become fixtures that are incorporated into Debtors' real property. Wells Fargo admits that it does not have a mortgage, or claim any other security interest in Debtors' real property, so if the windows have become fixtures, Wells Fargo's claim is unsecured.

* * *

Kansas courts have imposed a three-part test for determining if personal property has become a fixture, and thus part of the real estate. The three parts of the test are: (1) annexation to the realty (how firmly the items are attached and how easily they can be removed); (2) the intent of the parties (whether they intended the item to be permanently affixed to the real estate); and (3) how operation of the goods is related to the use of the realty (adaptability). All three requirements must be met before property will be deemed to be a fixture under Kansas law. In other words, "before personal property can become a fixture by actual physical annexation, the intention of the parties and the uses for which the personal property is to be put must all combine to change its nature from that of the chattel to that of the fixture."

The burden of proving that an item remains personal property lies with the party claiming the item is, in fact, personal property.[1] Thus, Wells Fargo has the burden of showing that the window are personal property by establishing that at least one of the three prongs of the above test are not met under the relevant facts.

Wells Fargo claims that the second prong of this test—the intent of the parties—establishes that the windows did not become fixtures but, instead, remained personal property. According to Wells Fargo, the parties' shared intent was for the windows to remain personal property, and that this Court should enforce that expressed intent. Alternatively, Debtors claim that all three parts of the test have been met, and the windows are now a fixture. As to the second part of the test, Debtors essentially argue that although they did agree that the windows would not become a fixture, that the Court cannot enforce that agreement because the parties cannot contractually agree to override the definition of a fixture.

Although at first blush it seems that windows in a home would typically be considered fixtures, there is precedent for the holding that parties can agree to treat property, which would otherwise qualify as fixtures, as personal property. For example, this issue was recently decided by a bankruptcy court in Arkansas, in *In re Williams*,[2] which applied identical contractual language from the same creditor involved here in deciding whether a guttering system at-

---

1. *Stalcup v. Detrich*, 27 Kan.App.2d 880, 886–87, 10 P.3d 3 (2000) (holding that a metal building attached by metal bolts to a concrete slab, with steel girders connected to each bolt, and sheeting attached to the steel girders, was personal property because (a) it could be removed although "it would take some effort" and removal would not cause damage to the real estate, (b) it was not particularly adapted to the farmland on which it sat, and (c) the owners' intention at the time of annexation for it to remain personal property was borne out by their provisions that it be separately taxed and that the taxes be paid by a distinct party).

2. *In re Williams*, 381 B.R. 742 (Bankr.W.D.Ark.2008). *See also* 35A Am.Jur.2d Fixtures § 19 (stating that "[t]he characterization put upon articles as fixtures or non-fixtures by parties to a purchase contract should be upheld where the rights of third parties are not adversely affected, no statute suggests a contrary result, and the articles are not so completely merged with the realty as to prevent removal of the article without material injury to the realty.")

tached to debtor's house should be considered a fixture or personal property. Wells Fargo claimed a security interest in the guttering system after using the same financing application and charge slip forms that were signed by Dalebout in this case. Williams claimed the guttering system had become a fixture in which Wells Fargo had no security interest.

The court examined numerous cases and secondary authorities that addressed the issue of whether the parties' intent, as evidenced by a contractual agreement, can transform what would ordinarily be considered a fixture into personal property. It concluded that the intent of the parties should control. The court held that as between the debtor and this particular creditor, their shared agreement that the gutters should remain household goods rather than fixtures was binding.

The court did express two caveats to this holding. First, it noted that the agreement is not binding on third parties without knowledge of the agreement. Second, it held that the intent of the parties may be overridden if removal of the items in question would cause extensive damage to the realty. [Although a bankruptcy court will recognize that an agreement between a debtor and creditor would be binding in an action between only those two parties, it nevertheless [would grant] the trustee's avoidance action because he was a third party.]

* * *

Wells Fargo cites to the Charge Slip, which was signed by Dalebout. It specifically states "You agree that any property described in this charge slip will remain personal property and will not become a fixture even if attached to real property." According to Wells Fargo, the Charge Slip conclusively establishes that the parties agreed that the windows would not become fixtures. Wells Fargo also claims that it relied on this agreement by not taking a mortgage on Dalebout's residence or otherwise attempting to perfect a security interest in Dalebout's real estate or fixtures. Debtors do not provide any evidence to refute Wells Fargo's arguments regarding intent.

The only remaining issue, then, is whether the removal of the windows would substantially damage the real estate. The parties' stipulation, which they agreed constituted all the evidence required for the Court to decide this case, is completely silent on any claim by Debtors that removal of the windows would cause damage to the real property.

Notwithstanding that there are no facts upon which this Court could find damage would be caused by the windows' removal, Wells Fargo generally noted in its brief that because these were replacement windows, no substantial damage to the real estate would occur with their removal. It argues that replacement windows are, by their very nature, removable and replaceable, and that the windows that were originally built with the house have already been removed and replaced with the windows in question, presumably without causing substantial damage to the house. It then argues that the current windows could similarly be removed without causing any additional damage to the house.

* * *

CONCLUSION

The Court finds that — as between Debtors and Wells Fargo — the windows in question are not considered fixtures but remained the personal property of Debtors, subject to Wells Fargo's purchase money security interest. As such, the Court finds that Wells Fargo does have a security interest in the replacement windows installed in Debtors' home, and its secured proof of claim was properly filed.

The Court again wishes to stress that its holding today is limited to the facts of the case before it. The Court is not generally holding that replacement windows can never become fixtures or do not typically become part of the real estate to which they are attached. Rather, the basis for this decision is the finding that the parties clearly agreed to treat the windows as personal property, an agreement on which Wells Fargo relied when determining what steps were necessary to protect its security interest in the property. Although the agreement between the parties is not binding on any third party without notice of the agreement, it is binding as between the only two parties to this particular dispute, Debtors and Wells Fargo.

Questions

Problem 5.1

➤ In taking a PMSI, what was Wells Fargo attempting to do?

Problem 5.2

➤ Assuming the debtor's residence was subject to a mortgage, would the mortgage holder have a claim superior to the claim of Wells Fargo?

Problem 5.3

➤ What if the windows were the originally installed windows, or if replacement windows were installed prior to the debtor's purchase of the property? Which party would prevail?

➤ Would the original supplier of windows (such as Home Depot) have priority over the mortgage holder assuming they had not been paid?

Problem 5.4

➤ If the replacement windows become fixtures, is a UCC #1 filing sufficient to protect Wells Fargo against third party claims?

Problem 5.5

➤ Look at the three prongs of the test used to determine if personal property has become a fixture. Is the court correct when it stated "Wells Fargo [must establish] that at least one of the three prongs of the above test are not met under the relevant facts?" If so, what do you make of the court later discussing damage to the real estate?

Problem 5.6

➤ Can Wells Fargo, by establishing the intent of the parties, protect itself against third party claims?

Problem 5.7

➤ If Wells Fargo may remove the windows as the Court suggests, does it have a duty to repair any damage to the real estate?

Problem 5.8

➤ The court quoted with approval a holding that an agreement between a debtor and a creditor agreeing that personalty would not become a fixture if third parties had knowledge of the agreement. Is that a correct statement of the law?

Problem 5.9

➤ How does Georgia deal with the issue of determining when a manufactured or mobile home becomes part of the real estate? *See,* O.C.G.A. § 8-2-181 and read the next case.

In re Smith

2008 WL 7390623 (Bankr. S.D. Ga. 2008)
(edited; most footnotes omitted)

DALIS, Bankruptcy Judge

ORDER ON OBJECTION TO SALE

This matter is before me on the objection by Atlantic Southern Bank ("Atlantic Southern") to the proposed sale by the chapter 7 Trustee of a large gilt and crystal chandelier ("Chandelier") that hung for an indeterminate period of time in the foyer of the former home of Debtors Marvin B. Smith and Sharon H. Smith. Atlantic Southern argues that the Chandelier is a fixture that Atlantic Southern owns as a result of having bought the Smiths' former home at foreclosure, even though the Chandelier had been removed before the fore-closure sale. The Trustee argues that the Chandelier is personalty that should be sold at auction with other assets of the bankruptcy estate for the benefit of creditors. The Trustee is correct, for the reasons that follow.

BACKGROUND

In May 2003, the Smiths, in order to finance the construction of their now-former home on Sea Island, Georgia (the "Sea Island Cottage"), executed a promissory note and a Deed to Secure Debt ("Security Deed"). The Security Deed conveyed the real property on which the Sea Island Cottage was to be built to a bank that later assigned the Security Deed to Atlantic Southern. The Security Deed covered "all existing and future improvements, structures, fix-tures, and replacements that may now, or at any time in the future, be part of the real estate described above."

Some time after the execution of the promissory note and the Security Deed, the Smiths bought the Chandelier. According to Mrs. Smith's unrefuted testi-mony at the hearing on this matter, no proceeds of the construction loan were used to buy it. The Smiths bought the Chandelier in Atlanta, and it was hung in the Sea Island Cottage by Mrs. Smith's brother after construction was com-plete. Installation consisted of clipping the Chandelier onto the wires from the junction box and hanging it by the chain.

Mrs. Smith also testified that the purpose of the Chandelier was decora-tive, as recessed ceiling lights already existed in the area where the Chande-lier was hung. Further, she testified that the Smiths had bought other chandeliers over the years and routinely moved them around from one home to another.

On April 2, 2007, the Smiths filed a chapter 11 bankruptcy case, which was later converted to a case under chapter 7. Atlantic Southern received stay re-lief and foreclosed on the Sea Island Cottage, buying it as the highest bidder at the foreclosure sale on May 6, 2008. At some point before the sale, the Smiths removed the Chandelier and took it with some furniture and decorative ac-cessories to an auction house in South Carolina. Mrs. Smith testified that the Chandelier was easily detached from the ceiling by unclipping the wires and un-hooking the chain and that its removal caused no damage.

The Trustee proposes to sell the Chandelier with the other items of per-sonalty at auction. Atlantic Southern objects, arguing that the Chandelier was a fixture covered under the Security Deed and that the Smiths had no right to remove it from the Sea Island Cottage. Atlantic Southern further argues that because the Chandelier as a fixture became part of the realty, the Chandelier now belongs to Atlantic Southern as a result of its purchase of the Sea Island Cottage at the foreclosure sale.

DISCUSSION

The question of whether the Chandelier is a fixture is determined under Georgia statutory and case law. If the Chandelier is a fixture, it was covered under the Security Deed; it became part of the realty when the Smiths hung it in the foyer of the Sea Island Cottage; the Smiths had no legal right to remove it; and Atlantic Southern now owns it as the purchaser of the realty at the foreclosure sale. If the Chandelier is personalty, it was not covered under the Security Deed; it belonged first to the Smiths and now to the bankruptcy estate; and it may be sold for the benefit of the creditors. Under Georgia law, the Chandelier is personalty.

I. The Georgia Law of Fixtures

Under the Code of Georgia, "[a]nything which is intended to remain permanently in its place even if it is not actually attached to the land is a fixture which constitutes a part of the realty and passes with it." Ga.Code Ann. §44-1-6. Courts determine whether a particular article has become realty or remains personalty by applying a multi-factor test incorporating rules of case law that date back as much as 150 years.

Georgia case law applying the law of fixtures specifically to chandeliers and other forms of lighting is limited to two landlord-tenant cases that are both more than a century old. See Wolff v. Sampson, 123 Ga. 400, 51 S.E. 335 (Ga.1905) (holding that gas fixtures were substitutes for lamps or candle stands and thus were personalty that could be removed by a tenant); Raymond v. Strickland, 124 Ga. 504, 52 S.E. 619 (Ga.1905) (holding that a chandelier was personalty that could be removed by the tenant).

The particular holdings, however, are of less interest and importance than the rule in Wolff that has survived:

> Whether an article of personalty connected with or attached to realty becomes a part of the realty, and therefore such a fixture that it cannot be removed therefrom, depends upon the circumstances under which the article was placed upon the realty, the uses to which it is adapted, and the parties who are at issue as to whether such an article is realty or detachable personalty.

Wolff, 51 S.E. at 335–36 (cited in, e.g., In re Hillis, No. 97-42591, 1998 WL 34064501, at *4 (Bankr.S.D.Ga. July 30, 1998) (holding that a canopy bed was personalty)).

A simpler rule has endured from a case decided even earlier than *Wolff*, in the mid-nineteenth century: "[W]herever the article can be removed without essential injury to the freehold, or the article itself, it is a chattel; otherwise, it is a fixture." *Wade v. Johnston*, 25 Ga. 331, 1858 WL 1963, at *3 (1858) (cited in, e.g., *Homac Inc. v. Fort Wayne Mortgage Co.*, 577 F.Supp. 1065, 1070 (N.D.Ga.1983) (holding that a mobile home did not become a fixture to the realty); *Tidwell v. Slocumb (In re Georgia Steel, Inc.)*, 71 B.R. 903, 911 (Bankr.M.D.Ga.1987) (holding that a radio tower was not a fixture)).

Present-day courts incorporate the rules from these historical cases into a multi-factor test that focuses on the parties' intent:

> Under Georgia law various factors should be considered in determining whether an article of personalty has become a part of the real property to which it has been actually or constructively annexed....

It is the *intent* of the parties ... which is the *primary* test in determining whether or not [the article] becomes a fixture.

Manderson & Assoc. v. Gore, 193 Ga.App. 723, 389 S.E.2d 251, 260 (Ga.Ct.App.1989). *See also Goger v. United States (In re Janmar, Inc.)*, 4 B.R. 4, *9 (Bankr.N.D.Ga.1979) ("The determination of whether or not an object has become a fixture is generally governed by the intent of the parties and is based upon a variety of factors.")

In addition to intent, courts consider such factors as whether the personalty and the realty share unity of title and, as in *Wade* 150 years ago, whether the article can be removed without causing damage to the article or to the realty. *See, e.g., Williamson v. Washington Mut. Home Loans, Inc. (In re Williamson)*, 387 B.R. 914, 920 (Bankr.M.D.Ga.2008). Courts also continue under *Wolff* to look at "the circumstances under which the article was placed upon the realty, the uses to which it is adapted, and the parties who are at issue." *See, e.g., In re Janmar*, 4 B.R. 4, *9 (Bankr.N.D.Ga.1979) (citing *Wolff*,.)

The multi-factor test permits individual factors to be given varying weight according to the circumstances of the case. *Manderson (citing 36A C.J.S. Fixtures § 1). If the parties' intention is difficult to discern, detachability of the article becomes important and has been held to be determinative.* See In re Georgia Steel, 71 B.R. at 911.

Under the circumstances here, I consider the parties' intention, the detachability of the Chandelier, and the use to which the Chandelier is adapted to determine whether it is a fixture or personalty.

II. The Chandelier is Personalty

A. Intent

Before this dispute arose, the parties did not express an intention as to whether the Chandelier would be considered a fixture, and they do not agree on an intention now. There was no expression of the parties' intention as to the Chandelier when the Security Deed was executed, the Chandelier not having been purchased at that time. The Security Deed provides only that "fixtures" would become part of the realty, without further elaboration or definition of that term. Mrs. Smith's testimony established that it was never the Smiths' intention for the Chandelier to become a permanent part of the realty and thus never their intention that the Chandelier should be considered a fixture. The Smiths did not communicate their intention to Atlantic Southern, however, just as Atlantic Southern did not communicate its intention as to what specifically would constitute a "fixture" until this dispute arose.

There being no expression or agreement about the parties' intention, that factor does not weigh in either direction in my determination. Consequently, whether the Chandelier is a fixture depends on its detachability and the use to which it is adapted. Both these factors weigh in favor of the Chandelier as personalty.

B. Detachability

Unrefuted testimony established that the Chandelier was easily detachable and in fact was detached without any injury to the Chandelier or to the Sea Island Cottage. The nature of the Chandelier's attachment thus was such that the Chandelier did not become a permanent part of the Sea Island Cottage, unlike the chandelier in a case under Louisiana law that Atlantic Southern cites, *Equibank v. IRS*, 749 F.2d 1176 (5th Cir.1985). In *Equibank*, the internal wiring of the house and the wiring of the chandeliers had to be professionally disconnected:

> Persons effecting the safe removal had to have sufficient knowledge of electricity and electrical wiring to separate the internal wires from the unit wires without risking harm to the worker, or damage to the house and fixtures by the touching of exposed wires or the "shorting out" of the circuitry. *This type removal is not comparable to the simple and ordinary unplugging of a lamp or other electrical appliance from a wall socket.*

Id. at 1177 (emphasis added).

Here, however, the Chandelier had not been wired into the electrical system of the Sea Island Cottage; it had simply been clipped in by Mrs. Smith's brother, who was not represented to have any electrical knowledge or training. Removing the Chandelier thus did not require separating or cutting any wires, but only unclipping the connection. This type of removal is comparable to unplugging a lamp and similarly can be accomplished "by persons with little or no knowledge of electricity," *Id.* at 1179. Accordingly, the detachability factor weighs in favor of the Chandelier as personalty.

C. Use to Which the Chandelier Is Adapted

Mrs. Smith's testimony established that the purpose of the Chandelier was decorative, the foyer being illuminated already with recessed ceiling lights. Consequently, with the Chandelier removed, a person standing in the foyer of the Sea Island Cottage can still "expect the room to become illuminated when the light switch is thrown," *Equibank*, 749 F.2d at 1180.

Because the Chandelier's purpose was decorative, not functional, this matter is not analogous to *Brooks v. John Hancock Mut. Life Ins. Co.*, 36 Ga.App. 261, 136 S.E. 166 (Ga.Ct.App.1926), a case cited by Atlantic Southern as "factually identical" (Atlantic Southern's Br. 3). Atlantic Southern is correct that both here and in *Brooks*, the parties are a mortgagor and a mortgagee that later bought the realty at foreclosure; and that the mortgagor attached items of personalty to the realty after the execution of the security deed. The items the purchaser sought to recover in *Brooks*, however, were "a steam engine, boiler, and gin outfit." 136 S.E. 166. This machinery is not "like the chandelier in our case" (Atlantic Southern's Br. 3).

Atlantic Southern says that in *Brooks*, the mortgagor installed the equipment "to carry out the obvious purpose for which the building was erected" and asserts that the Smiths installed the Chandelier for the same reason. (Atlantic Southern's Br. 3.) This comparison is inapt. In *Brooks*, the purpose for which the building was erected was industrial, and machinery is essential to industrial operations. In contrast, the Sea Island Cottage is a residence, and an object purchased for decorative effect, like the Chandelier, is not essential to a residential purpose.

The matter here also is not like the case that Atlantic Southern incorrectly asserts is controlling precedent, *Tifton Corp. v. Decatur Fed. Sav. & Loan Assoc.*, 136 Ga.App. 710, 222 S.E.2d 115 (Ga.Ct.App.1975). *Tifton* involved stoves and refrigerators installed in each of the units in an apartment complex. *Id.* at 116. The court characterized these appliances as "trade fixtures attached to the purpose for which the building was constructed." *Id.* at 117. The apartment units could not have been rented without stoves and refrigerators. These items thus were essential to the purpose of the realty. The Chandelier, in contrast, is not a trade fixture and is not essential to the purpose of the realty, as explained in the discussion of *Brooks*, above.

Further, in *Tifton* there was "absolutely no testimony to show that the stoves and refrigerators were not installed in and attached to the property so as to become a part of the realty." *Id.* at 116–17. Here, Mrs. Smith's unrefuted' testimony established that the Chandelier was not attached to the Sea Island Cottage in such a way that the Chandelier became part of the realty.

Brooks and *Tifton* show that when items of personalty with a functional, essential purpose are attached to realty, the items will be considered fixtures. The Chandelier's decorative purpose places it outside the rule in these cases. Accordingly, the use to which the Chandelier is adapted weighs in favor of the Chandelier as personalty.

CONCLUSION

Considering the intention of the parties, the detachability of the Chandelier, and the use to which it is adapted, I conclude that under Georgia law, the Chandelier is personalty. It follows that the Chandelier was not covered under the Security Deed; it belonged first to the Smiths and now to the bankruptcy estate; and it may be sold for the benefit of the creditors. The Objection to Sale filed by Atlantic Southern Bank is therefore *ORDERED OVERRULED.*

Questions

Problem 5.10

➤ How would you contrast the replacement windows described in *In re Dalebout* with the chandelier in *In re Smith*?

➤ Is there a subjective or objective test?

B. Introduction to Default

Section 9-601 to 9-628 governs the "Default and Enforcement of Security Interest." In analyzing and complying with the procedures contained therein, the following should be kept in mind as a guide to a secured party's actions:

a.   The contractual provisions that define (the security agreement) are subject to the duty of good faith, unconscionability defenses, and waiver of rights, if any.

b.   The secured creditor may acquire the collateral, §9-604, and seek any deficiency under the monetary obligation signed by the obligor or sue directly on the monetary obligation or keep the collateral in full payment of the obligation under the conditions set forth in §9-620(a).

   c.   If using self-help, the secured creditor may not breach the peace. *See,* §9-609(b)(2).

   d.   Any sale of collateral, whether public or private must be commercially reasonable after appropriate notice to interested parties. *See,* §9-611.

Sections 9-613 and 9-614 contain sample forms to be used by a secured creditor when disposing of the collateral.

1. Default

Contractual provisions specifying in what constitutes default are subject to §1-103 including when a contract provision is unconscionable. *See,* also §9-102(a)(43) (§9-102(a)(44) in the Georgia version of Art 9).

Questions

Problem 5.11

➢ What might a contract include as an event of default giving a secured creditor the right to accelerate the amount due and repossess the collateral?

Problem 5.12

➢ Why do creditors include an acceleration clause allowing all payments to become immediately due and payable after a default?

Problem 5.13

➢ Is a contract clause providing for an acceleration of the debt if the secured party deems itself as insecure enforceable?

➢ Under what circumstances?

Problem 5.14

➢ What if the debtor changes jobs? *See, Sheppard Federal Credit Union v. Palmer,* 408 F.2d 1369 (5th Cir 1996).

Problem 5.15

➢ What if the debtor is known to have consulted a bankruptcy attorney? *See, Fort Knox Bank v. Gustafson,* 385 S.W.2d 196 (1996).

2. Seeking Payment under the Monetary Obligation

Example and Questions

Assume that a party secured by the Debtor's automobile repossesses the automobile as a result of the Debtor's default in payment. The secured party accelerates the debt making the Debtor liable for a total balance owed of $18,000. The automobile is sold in a commercially reasonable sale as required by §9-610(a)(b). Sections 9-608 and 9-607(a)(2) provide for the application of proceeds from a secured party's sale of collateral.

Questions

Problem 5.16

➤ If the best available exchange for the automobile is a note with a face value of $15,000, is the secured party required to immediately credit the Debtor with that amount? *See,* §9-608(a)(3).

Problem 5.17

➤ Assume that the automobile is sold in a private sale that is commercially reasonable and in compliance with §9-611 (appropriate notification to the Debtor). In exchange, the secured party gets chattel paper consistent with its usual business practices. Should the secured party immediately credit the Debtor's account?

➤ Is the value equal to the face amount?

Under both above scenarios, the Debtor still owes money after applying the proceeds as required by §9-615. Note that §9-616 controls the secured party's responsibility to explain the allocation of the proceeds from the disposition of collateral. Note the rule applicable to consumer obligations in §9-616(b) which should be read with §9-625 which provides for "Remedies for Secured Party's failure to Comply with Article." *See,* Comment 4 to §9-625 dealing with minimum damages in consumer-goods transactions.

Problem 5.18

➤ Assume the automobile repossessed by the secured party was subject to a lien or security interest subordinate to the secured party's. What obligation does the repossessing creditor have? *See,* §§9-611(b)(c), 9-615(a)(3)(4), (b).

Problem 5.19

➤ What if the repossessed collateral is subject to a lien or security interest superior to the interest of the repossessing secured party? *See,* §9-617.

Sections 9-620 and 9-621 deal with strict foreclosure, a "procedure by which the secured party acquires the Debtor's interest in the collateral without the need for a sale or other disposition under Section 9-610." *See,* Comment 2 to §9-620. Note that these sections are subject to the obligation of good faith.

See, Comment 11 to §9-620. Note, also, the special rules for consumer cases. *See,* §9-620(e)(f)(g) and Comment 12 to §9-620.

3. Breach of the Peace

What constitutes a breach of the peace is decided on a case by case basis. *See generally, Dobbs' Georgia Enforcement of Security Interests in Personal Property Under Revised Article 9 with Forms.*

Lewis v. Nicholas Financial, Inc., 686 S.E.2d 468 (Ga. App. 2009), involved an independent contractor for a secured creditor. The court, in overruling *Johnson v. First Union National Bank,* 567 S.E.2d 44 (Ct. App. Ga. 2002), held that the statutory duty in §9-609(b)(2) not to breach the peace is non-delegable.

The court pointed out that someone employing an independent contractor is not generally liable for any torts committed, but this rule does not apply "if the wrongful act breaches a duty imposed upon the employee by statute," citing O.C.G.A. §51-2-5(4). *Id.* at 470. The court further held that it was "immaterial whether [the secured creditor] was negligent in its own right." *Id.* Section 51-2-5 provides:

Employer liable for negligence of contractor, when

An employer is liable for negligence of a contractor:

(1) When the work is wrongful in itself or, if done in the ordinary manner, would result in a nuisance;

(2) If, according to the employer's previous knowledge and experience, the work to be done is in its nature dangerous to others however carefully performed;

(3) If the wrongful act is the violation of a duty imposed by express contract upon the employer;

(4) If the wrongful act is the violation of a duty imposed by statute;

(5) If the employer retains the right to direct or control the time and manner of executing the work or interferes and assumes control so as to create the relation of master and servant or so that an injury results which is traceable to his interference; or

(6) If the employer ratifies the unauthorized wrong of the independent contractor.

Appendix A

Approaching Article 9 Analytically

Remember that Article 9 is all about a secured party taking an interest in personal property to secure payment of an obligation, that is, the secured party wants to get paid. If the obligator fails to pay as agreed, then the secured party has the option of recovering what he can through exercising his rights in the collateral.

First: Identify the parties involved.
1. Merchant
2. Non-merchant businessman
3. Farmer
4. Consumer
5. Secured Party
6. Lien Creditor

Second: Identify the collateral.
1. Tangible
2. Quasi-Tangible
3. Intangible
4. Sui generis. Examples include:
   a. Deposit Accounts
   b. Chattel Paper. If assignable treat as if a quasi-tangible
   c. Investment property

Third: Determine whether the collateral is original or proceeds of other collateral. If proceeds may the automatically perfected secured party be primed by another secured party giving value in good faith as part of his business. Note particularly when the proceeds are quasi-tangible or qualify as sui generis.

Fourth: Determine if the secured party's interest is perfected and, if so,
1. Automatically
2. By Filing
3. By Possession
4. By Control
5. Or is Subject to a Certificate of Title Statute

Fifth: Determine the priority of the secured party.
1. First in time first in right from the time of perfection or filing is the general rule
2. Determine if there is there a relation back effect for perfection
   a. Does first to file a Financing Statement control if there are competing secured creditors whose interests have attached rather than time of attachment?
   b. Is the security interest a PMSI which, if in equipment or consumer goods, has a 20 day relation back effect to the time of attachment and the debtor's possession for perfection by filing?
   c. Is there an exception to the first to perfect rule such as for a PMSI in equipment or inventory which, if proper procedures are followed, primes a previously perfected interest that floats over all inventory or covers equipment in general.
   d. Is there an exception to the first to perfect rule if the collateral is freely transferable such as by possession or control giving the party who takes in good faith in the ordinary course of his business for value an interest superior to the secured party who relied on filing?

Sixth: Determine if the personal property securing the debt has become a fixture subject to real estate law.

Appendix B

Summary Collateral Index— 2001 Version of the U.C.C.

Personal property used as collateral is characterized generally as tangible (goods), quasi-tangible (documents and instruments that embody the right to property including the payment of money—reification) or intangible (personal property that has no physical manifestation, such as accounts or contracts which are evidence of a right).

Personal property not easily characterized in any of the above categories including chattel paper, both in tangible (9-102(a)(78), 9-102(a)(77) in Georgia or in electronic form (9-102(a)(31), 9-102(a)(32) in Georgia, deposit accounts (9-102(a)(29), 9-102(a)(30), in Georgia, commercial tort claims (9-102(a)(13), 9-102(a)(14) in Georgia, investment property (9-102(a)(49), 9-102(a)(50) in Georgia which may be certificated (8-102), uncertificated (8-102), constitute a securities entitlement (8-102) or be a securities account (8-501), commodity account (9-102(a)(15), and letter of credit rights (9-102-(a)(51), 9-102(a)(52) in Georgia.

Code references are to the current UCC Article 9. As enacted in Georgia and other states those references may vary slightly as set- forth above.

Goods	UCC Reference
General Definition	9-102 (a) (44)
Consumer Goods	9-102 (a) (23)
Equipment	9-102 (a) (33)
Inventory	9-102 (a) (48)
Farm Product	9-102 (a) (34)
Fixtures	9-102 (a) (41)

Other classifications for goods includes as—extracted collateral (9-102 (a) (6) software (9-102 (a) (25), and accessions (9-102 (a) (1).

Each of the above is subject to rules governing perfection and priority. Certain goods whether classified as consumer goods or equipment such as automobiles may be subject to statutes other than Art. 9 with regard to perfection and priority (*see*, 9-102(a) (10).

Quasi-tangibles (sometimes Quasi-intangibles)

	UCC Reference
Documents	9-102(a)(30)
(negotiable & non-negotiable)	
Instruments	9-102(a) (47)
	UCC Article 3 defines
	Instruments as negotiable
(a) Drafts and checks	UCC Articles 3 & 4
(b) Promissory Notes	See 9-102(a)(65)
	Georgia 9-109(a)(3)
Intangibles	9-102(a)(42)
(a) Account	9-102(a)(2) & 9-109(a)(3)
(b) Payment Intangibles	9-102(a)(61) & 9-102(a)(60)
(c) Health Care Receivables	9-102(a)(46) & 9-109(d)(8)
Chattel Paper	
(a) Tangible	9-102(a)(78) & 9-301(3)
(b) Electronic	9-102(a)(31) & 9-105
Deposit Account	
Definition and	9-102(a)(29), 9-104
Enforceability of a Security Interest	9-109(d)(10)(a)
	9-203(b)(3)(1)
Commercial Tort Claims	
(a) Definition	9-102(a)(13)
(b) Description	9-108(e)(1)
(c) Limits	9-204(b)(2)
Investment Property	
(a) Definitions	9-102(a)(49), 8-501
(b) Enforceability of Security Interest	9-106(a), 9-203(b)(3)(c)(d)
Interest	9-314(c)(2)(b), 9-331

Commodity Contracts

    (a) Definition   9-102(a)(15), 9-108(d)(2)

    (b) Enforceability of Security Interest   9-106(b)(c)

Letter of Credit Rights

    (a) Definition   9-102(a)(51)

    (b) Enforceability of Security Interest   9-107, 9-109 (c)(4)

                                      9-203(b)(3)(d)

Appendix C

Uniform Commercial Code And Georgia Selected Article 9 Non-Uniform Variations

U.C.C. Section	Georgia Variation
§9-102(a)	Adds §9-102(a)(8)
	"(8) 'Authority' means the Georgia Superior Court Clerks' Cooperative Authority."
§9-102(a)(11)	Renumbered §9-102(a)(12) which omits "a security interest in specific goods and license of software used in the goods" before, "a lease of specific goods".
§9-102(a)(44)	Renumbered §9-102(a)(45) which omits "(v) manufactured homes."
§9-102(a)(53)	§9-102(a)(53) not adopted.
§9-102(a)(54)	§9-102(a)(54) not adopted.
§9-102(a)(55)	Renumbered §9-102(a)(54) adding a second sentence: "The term includes a deed to secure debt."
§9-102(a)(67)(B)	Renumbered §9-102(a)(66)(B) replacing "20 years" with "5 years."
§9-109(d)(11)	§9-109(d)(11) adds "or usufruct" before "or rents thereunder."
§9-109(d)	§9-109(d), "Inapplicability of article" subsections (14), adds an assignment of a lottery prize; (15) an assignment of a claim or right to receive payment pursuant to O.C.G.A. §34-9-84, Worker's Compensation, or by

	Article 5 of Chapter 12 of Title 51, Tort Damages for Injury.
§9-111	§9-111 added providing that "the creation of a security interest is not a bulk transfer...."
§9-210(f)	§9-210(f) replaces $25 with $10.
§9-301(3)(C)	Subsection (C) is omitted and subsection (D) is renumbered as (C).
§9-309(14)	§9-309(14) not adopted. This subsection refers to the "lottery or other game of chance."
§9-317(d)	§9-317(d) omits "electronic documents" before "general intangibles."
§9-323(b)	§9-323(b) not-adopted.
§9-323(c)	§9-323(b) is (c) in the U.C.C. and replaces "Subsections (a) and (b) do not apply ..." with "Subsection (a) of this Code section does not apply...."
§9-333	§9-333 is a complete re-write of U.C.C. §9-333 and is appended herein as Appendix C.
§9-334(e)(4)	§9-334(e)(4) not adopted dealing with manufactured homes.
§9-334(i)	§9-334(i) adds "or agricultural lien upon...."
§9-334(j)	§9-334(j) not adopted.
§9-406(j)	§9-406(j) not adopted.
§9-408(c)	§9-408(c) adds "Except as otherwise provided in Code Section 53-12-80," dealing with the "Validity of spend thrift provisions."
§9-501(a)(1)(A)	§9-501(a)(1)(A) adds "growing crops" after "collateral."
§9-501(a)(2)	§9-501(a)(2) designates the filing office as the "office of the clerk of the superior court of any county."
§9-501(b)	§9-501(b) same as to the filing office.
§9-502(a)	§9-502(a)(4) provides: "Where both (A) the collateral described consists only of consumer goods as defined in paragraph (24) of subsection (a) of Code Section 11-9-102 and (B) the secured obligation is originally $5,000.00 or less, gives the maturity date of the secured obligation or specifies that such obligation is not subject to a maturity date."

§9-502(b)	§9-502(b) adds "growing crop" after "collateral."
§9-502(b)(2) and (3)	§9-502(b)(2) and (3) adopts the bracketed language.
§9-512(a)	§9-512(a) adopts alternative A for amending financing statements.
§9-513(c)	§9-513(c) rewritten as follows: *Other collateral.* In cases not governed by subsection (a) of this Code section, within 90 days after there is no obligation, or otherwise give value or, if earlier, within 20 days after a secured party receives an authenticated demand from a debtor, the secured party shall cause the secured party of record for a financing statement to send to the debtor a termination statement for the financing statement or file the termination statement in the filing office if:
§9-513(d)	§9-513(d) omits the final sentence dealing with utilities.
§9-514(c)	§9-514(c) not adopted dealing with assignments of a security interest.
§9-515(a)	§9-515(a) replaces "subsections (b), (e), (f), (g)" with "subsection (d) of this Code section."
§9-515(b)	§9-515(b) not adopted dealing with public financed and manufactured homes.
§9-515(e)	§9-515(d) after: "absence of the filing", adds "or, where both (1) the collateral described consists only of consumer goods as defined in paragraph (24) of subsection (a) of Code Section 11-9-102 and (2) the secured obligation is originally $5,000.00 or less, any earlier maturity date of the secured obligation specified on such continuation statement." In the second sentence, adds "or the earlier occurrence of a required specified maturity date."
§9-515(f) and (g)	§9-515(f) and (g) not adopted.
§9-516(b)(3)(D)	§9-516(b)(3)(D) adopts optional language which is bracketed on filing.
§9-516(b)(5)(C)(iii)	§9-516(b)(5)(C)(iii) not adopted as initial information on a financing statement.
§9-516(b)(7)	§9-516(b)(7) not adopted.
§9-518(b)	§9-518(b) adds: "The correction statement shall be filed in the filing office of the county where the record was filed."

§9-518(b)	§9-518(b) adopts alternative A on the sufficiency of a correction statement.
§9-519(a)(3)	§9-519(a)(3) rewritten to provide for record keeping by electronic means.
§9-519(a)(4)	§9-519(a)(4) sets forth a 24 hour requirement for transmitting records.
§9-519(b)	§9-519(b) not adopted.
§9-519(d)	§9-519(d) adds "crops" after "collateral"
§9-519(f)	§9-519(f) adopts alternative A on retrieval of information and rewrites introductory paragraph as follows: "Retrieval and association capability. The authority and each filing office shall maintain a capability with respect to the records they are required to index."
§9-519(h) and (i)	§9-519(h) not adopted.
§9-521	§9-521 expanded and written dealing with "Uniform Form of Written Financing Statement and Amendment." *See*, Appendix C.
§9-523	§9-523 adds "and central indexing system."
§9-523 to §9-526	§9-523 to §9-526 on administrative procedures are re-written.
§9-527	§9-527 not adopted deals with reporting duties of government officials.

Appendix D

Selected Reproduced Non-Uniform Variations

O.C.G.A. 11-9-333 (2010). Priority of certain liens.

(a) Year's support; property taxes; other state taxes; other taxes or judgments. Except as is expressly provided to the contrary elsewhere in this article and in subsection (b) of this Code section, a perfected security interest in collateral takes priority over each and all of the liens, claims, and rights described in Code Section 44-14-320, relating to the establishment of certain liens, as now or hereafter amended, and Code Section 53-7-91 of the "Pre-1998 Probate Code," if applicable, or Code Section 53-7-40 of the "Revised Probate Code of 1998," relating to the priority of debts against the estate of a decedent, as now or hereafter amended, provided, nevertheless, that:

(1) Year's support to the family, duly set apart in the collateral prior to the perfection of the subject security interest, takes priority over such security interest;

(2) A lièn for property taxes duly assessed upon the subject collateral, either prior or subsequent to the perfection of the subject security interest, takes priority over security interest;

(3) A lien for all other state taxes takes priority over such security interest, except where such security interest is perfected by filing a financing statement relative thereto prior to such time as the execution for such state taxes shall be entered on the execution docket in the place and in the manner provided by law; provided, nevertheless, that, with respect to priority rights between such tax liens and security interests where under this article the same are perfected other than by filing a financing statement, the same shall be determined as provided by law prior to January 1, 1964; and

(4) A lien for other unpaid taxes or a duly rendered judgment of a court having jurisdiction shall have the same priority with regard to a security interest as it would have if the tax lien or judgment were a conflicting security interest within the meaning of Code Section 11-9-322 or an encumbrance within the meaning of Code Section 11-9-334, which conflicting security interest was perfected by filing or which encumbrance arose at the time the tax lien or judgment was duly recorded in the place designated by statute applicable thereto.

(b) Mechanics' liens on farm machinery. A mechanics' lien on farm machinery or equipment arising on or after July 1, 1985, shall have priority over any perfected security interest in such farm machinery or equipment unless a financing statement has been filed as provided in Code Section 11-9-501 and unless the financing statement describes the particular piece of farm machinery or equipment to which the perfected security interest applies. Such description may include the make, model, and serial number of the piece of farm machinery or equipment. However, such description shall be sufficient whether or not it is specific if it reasonably identifies what is described and a mistake in such description shall not invalidate the description if it provides a key to identifying the farm machinery or equipment.

O.C.G.A. 11-9-521 (2010). Uniform form of written financing statement and amendment; authority may prescribe forms.

(a) Initial financing statement form. Except for a reason set forth in subsection (b) of Code Section 11-9-516, a filing office that accepts written records may not refuse to accept a written initial financing statement in the form and format set out in Section 9-521(a) of the Official Text of Revised Article 9, 2000 Revision, of the Uniform Commercial Code promulgated by the American Law Institute and the National Conference of Commissioners on Uniform State Laws, and such form and format are incorporated into this subsection by reference.

(b) Amendment form. Except for a reason set forth in subsection (b) of Code Section 11-9-516, a filing office that accepts written records may not refuse to accept a written record amending an initial financing statement if such record is in the form and format set out in Section 9-521(b) of the Official Text of Revised Article 9, 2000 Revision, of the Uniform Commercial Code promulgated by the American Law Institute and the National Conference of Commissioners on Uniform State Laws, and such form and format are incorporated into this subsection by reference.

(c) Authority's forms. The authority may prescribe forms for initial financing statements and amendments. Subject to the provisions of subsections
(a) and (b) of this Code section, all written financing statements and
amendments must be presented for filing on forms prescribed by the authority.

Appendix E

2010 Amendments to Article 9

As of May 22, 2012, twenty-six states had enacted the 2010 Amendments to Article 9 of the UCC that were drafted and approved by both the Uniform Law Commission and the American Law Institute in 2010. These states include:

- Colorado
- Connecticut
- Florida
- Hawaii
- Idaho
- Indiana
- Iowa
- Kansas
- Kentucky
- Maryland
- Michigan
- Minnesota
- Nebraska
- Nevada
- North Dakota
- Ohio
- Oregon
- Puerto Rico
- Rhode Island
- South Dakota
- Tennessee
- Texas

- Virginia
- Washington
- West Virginia
- Wisconsin

The 2010 Amendments were designed to provide greater guidance to naming the debtor on financing statements, improvements to the filing system for filing financing statements, and greater protection for existing secured parties when the debtor relocates to another state or merges with another entity.

UCC Index

Index